I would especially wish to credit James Gowan and Michael
Wilford, and the following architects who also have made
important contributions to the work of the office:

David Bartlett, Alfred Bews, Russ Bevington, Jorge Burga,
Roy Cameron, Kit Evans, David Falck, Brian Frost,
David Gibson, Julian Harrap, Malcolm Higgs, Gunter Ismer,
Leo Krier, Werner Kreis, Robert Livesey, Robin Nicholson,
Crispin Osborne, Peter Ray, Bryn Riches, Ueli Schaad,
Tony Smith, Quinlan Terry, David Walsby, David Weinberg.

The illustrations shown on pages 16, 17 and 23 were drawn by
James Gowan. Mr Gowan also drew the foreground for the
drawing on pages 24, 25.

JS.

The exhibition that accompanied this catalogue was made
possible by the generosity of Alistair McAlpine

Published by RIBA Publications Ltd
66 Portland Place, London W1N 4AD
in association with the RIBA Drawings Collection

ISBN: 0 900630 60 4

Printed by Unwin Brothers Limited,
The Gresham Press, Old Woking, Surrey

RIBA DRAWINGS COLLECTION

JAMES STIRLING

EXHIBITION

ROYAL INSTITUTE OF BRITISH ARCHITECTS

HEINZ GALLERY

21 PORTMAN SQUARE LONDON

24 APRIL—21 JUNE

1974

2ND EDITION

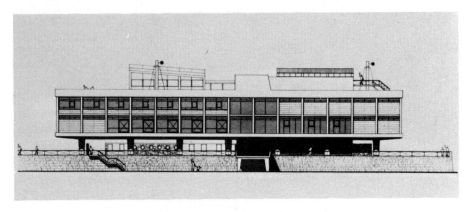

Thesis: A community centre in a new town
Liverpool University School of Architecture 1950

'He took the Mies Admin and Library building for I.I.T. and raised it up on Corbu style *pilotis.*
And it was all, as far as I was concerned, rather impressive for its facility and distinctly shocking
for its highly casual manipulation of derivations. But, of course, immediately and then and there, I
saw it as something American. *The land of the Noble Savage* had elicited or instilled this simplicity
of approach — and it was my conviction that this was the case which was an overwhelming reason
for bringing me to the U.S.

I think that it is without doubt that a certain number of students at Liverpool during the late
forties and very early fifties did feel themselves to be, in some quite important way, *avant garde;*
and I believe that I myself probably did have *something* to do with crystallizing this position . . .
Heroes were above all Corbu, various central European figures known from the earlier editions of
F. R. S. Yorke's *The Modern House* and *The Modern Flat,* Giuseppe Terragni — known from Mario
Labo's little book, and perhaps certain persons published by Sartoris — as for instance, Cesare
Cattaneo.

In fact, one believes that both Mannerist *angst* and Mannerist virtuosity were both quite a little bit
admired, and therefore, it does not seem entirely inappropriate that, when some of this work was
shown at the AA in the fall of '53 (including Jim's thesis), it was referred to by Astragal (Banham)
in the *Architects' Journal* as *maniera Liverpudliana.'*

From a letter by C. Rowe to J. Jacobus
(C. Rowe was Stirling's thesis tutor at Liverpool)

INTRODUCTION

Reyner Banham

Had James Stirling not lived beyond his twentyfifth birthday he might still be remembered in his generation as the man who introduced 'zip-a-tone' to Britain. It would be a disputable memory — Gordon Cullen, among others, has some right to the title — but it would still be an apt memory because the introduction of mechanical tints into presentation drawings is in character with much else that Stirling has contributed to British architecture.

The period — the very early fifties — was a time of craft professionalism on the one hand, or romantic expressionism on the other — Meyerscough-Walker's dazzling proficiency in reducing watercolour to a precise neutral medium, like pale Ektachrome, on the first hand, confronting Hugh Casson's jokes (or were they?) about 'this one I'm rendering in lipstick and paraffin on coarse sand-paper'. Both approaches, however, celebrated the manual skill of the delineator's craft; 'zip-a-tone' did not. What craft it contained in the cutting away of areas of film not required, was subtractive and self-concealing.

Coupled with the strong but fastidious quality of Stirling's ruled line, however, it gave an effect at once rich and mechanistic. At a time when the drawing style of his contemporaries tended to be determinedly but boringly neutral, in wishful emulation of a Mies van der Rohe image that never was, Stirling produced drawings that were powerful expressions of himself, and of the intended character of the buildings they represented (I recall, for example, the elaborately orchestrated side-elevation of the Sheffield University teaching block) without ever lapsing into the 'sympathetic magic of the personal touch'.

Not all his drawings of that epoch used mechanical tints, nor did they need to. The reason why 'zip-a-tone' worked so well for him (and so ill for some of his imitators) was that he was ready for it. Far from being an applied gimmick, it had qualities that his drawing style was developing anyhow. In this it somewhat resembled that later relationship of patent glazing to his built architecture. That, too, was a regular and mechanical surface coverage whose quality was not of the architect's making nor subject to his personal touch (unlike, alas, too much off-the-form concrete by others in that same epoch around 1966). Yet it has persistently been one of his most effective and personal architectural usages.

In this it has been more revealing of the man, I suspect, than the diagonally patterned pre-cast concrete at St Andrews. That represents a more literal relationship between graphic technique and architectural surface, something like the relationship of fine-ruled engravings and finely pick-tooled ashlar in Anglo-Palladian architecture of the eighteenth century. 'Zip-a-tone' and patent glazing however, reveal the man by denying him. Both are impersonal coverings that can say something important *for* Stirling without saying a thing *about* Stirling. And that is very much in character; as a creative personality· he plays his cards close to his chest, rather than wearing his heart on his sleeve. He puts before the public finished and perfected works, but does not invite us to admire or share in the creative process by way of preliminary sketches.

There is more truth than apparent rhetoric in Stirling's statement that 'some jobs are designed in the working drawings, there are no preliminary sketches'. One such working drawing, of a very specialised kind, is in fact well-known — the perspective of the 'cascading' glass between the stair-towers of the Leicester laboratories. And the importance of that drawing is that it explains the forms of that facetted fall of patent glazing as no other convention of presentation ever could. It says in a single image something that regular orthogonal projection could say only with less clarity and a multiplicity of images. The use of such non-orthogonal techniques by the Stirling office has been the subject of increasing commentary by the growing tribe of Stirlingoligists. Charles Jencks for instance has written enthusiastically

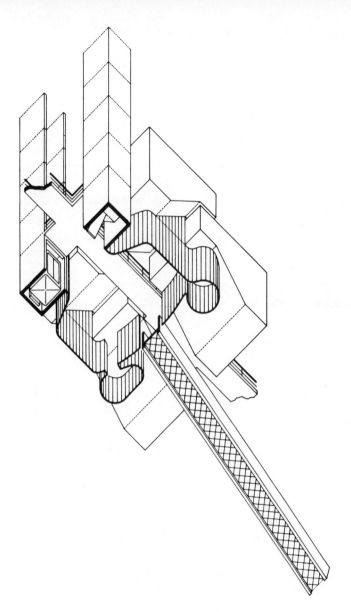

Sheffield University 1953

This view of part of the arts/administration building reveals several of the building (usage) elements which are put together in differing ways in the projects which came after — for instance the circulation armature i.e. vertical shafts (lifts and staircases) and the corridors as galleries. The approach ramp to entrance lobbies and the sloping undercut to lecture theatres also re-appear in later projects; as does the free-form glazing wall, which in this instance wraps around the space of the principal receiving area.

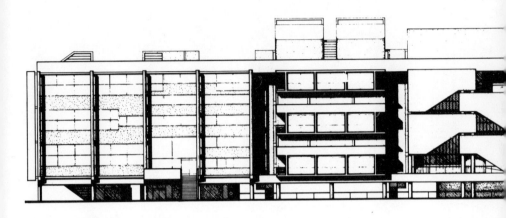

The structure bays are:
AAAABAABACACACABAABAAAA
the dimension of A is twice B, which is twice C.

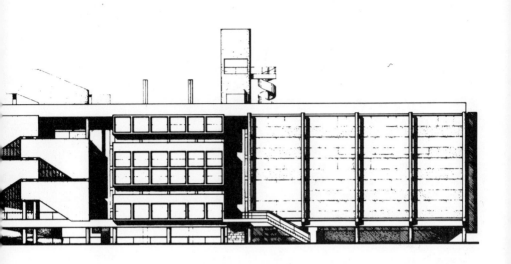

Sheffield University 1953

'At ground level the main building was a covered way linking buildings at either end of the site and, as the site sloped down into the town, it also had to act as a retaining wall to the campus. From left to right it included a School of Architecture, then a battery of classrooms; in the centre a cluster of lecture theatres, entered from two levels, then a group of staff rooms, and finally the University administration. Each of these groupings was separated by a shaft of vertical circulation — a recessive element which visually articulates the different types of accommodation. The horizontal circulation was regarded as a spine or driving axle on to which rooms were connected, like a mechanised assembly. The planning of spaces and rooms was secondary to the creation of a circulatory system.'

An architect's approach to architecture, RIBA Journal, May 1965 (if not always accurately) that 'Stirling's work is rooted in his technique of draughting; the method leads to the form. Without such a technique sophisticated constructions would be impossible.'

'A whole aesthetic and a way of life comes from the logic and articulation possible with such methods'. So says Jencks in the caption to axonometrics of Leicester, St Andrews, Dorman Long, the Florey building, and a perspective of a *Mariner* spacecraft. Alongside, in the main text of *Modern movements in architecture*, he concludes: 'If one were to characterise this architecture in a single phrase, it would be like the perspective of the lunar spacecraft; complex functions made manifest,' while the caption proper finishes by recalling that axonometric projection was 'incidentally used by all the architects in *British buildings*'.

Shrewd stuff, but destroyed by over-elaboration. The fact that standard axonometrics were used throughout *British buildings* (Kenneth Frampton's factional florilegium of friends' works) simply means that it is one of the simplest means of disciplining the presentation of widely differing buildings — precisely why it had been used back in the heroic period of modern architecture to discipline the illustrations in the catalogue of the Weissenhof exhibition.

In both cases it was used because it makes buildings look democratically equal without making them look alike or destroying their characteristic complexities — but, of itself, it implies nothing about their mode of design. The comparison with the spacecraft perspective also misleads, on two different grounds. Firstly, because the Mariner sequence were assemblies of separate functional modules connected apart (so to speak) by spars and struts, complex in their totality, rather than in the functions or their connections, whereas Stirling clearly needs to use axonometrics because he has to explicate assemblies of functions that are complex in themselves, and more complex in their interlocking than may appear at first sight. Secondly, it misleads precisely by being a perspective, and thus lacking the 'all-dimensions-true' quality that gives axonometrics their authority. Stirling

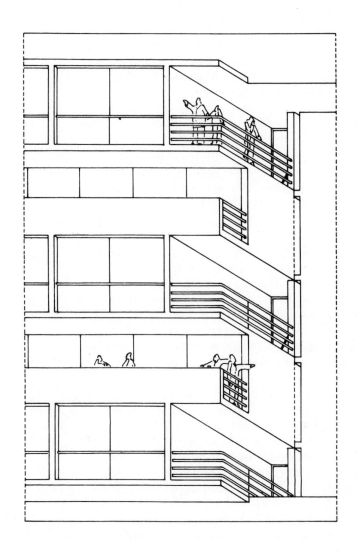

Sheffield University 1953

External detail of Seminar and tutorial rooms, fitted between recessed shafts of vertical circulation (lifts and staircase).

uses perspectives to explicate quite different aspects of his buildings from what is communicated by the kind of axonometrics he has made famous.

And if they are famous it is because they clearly have some value for Stirling that other means of presentation do not. He himself will explain in conversation how they clarify design decisions by making their consequences explicit. Some of his axonometrics don't seem to an outsider to do that very well (those of St Andrews, for instance) but they may have performed this useful service strictly within the context of the Stirling office, whereas other axonometrics, such as those of Leicester or the Florey building, have been spectacularly effective in presenting the true nature of these designs even to lay outsiders.

The value of these particular drawings is that they do indeed, as Jencks rightly points out, show 'the space, the structure, geometry, function and detail together without distortion.' It is for this reason above others that they can strike the outsider as such flashes of architectural revelation, and it is for related reasons that they perform their 'regulatory' function within the office — that is, at an appropriate stage in the design process (usually near the end), axonometrics are produced which make it possible to assess the total architectural consequences of design decisions made to date. However, it is very strikingly apparent that in spite of this seemingly tentative or experimental function, most of these drawings present the air of refined and finished works of art and are uncommonly like the buildings as built.

But they do not exist on their own; scholarly pre-occupation with Stirling's axonometrics seems to have obscured the observation that in nearly all cases of buildings with important interior spaces, the office prepares perspectives in the same immaculate technique, equally capable of standing on their own as works of art. And equally at variance with what is commonly conceived to be a presentation drawing they all tend to be too small, they do not ingratiate, and they remain

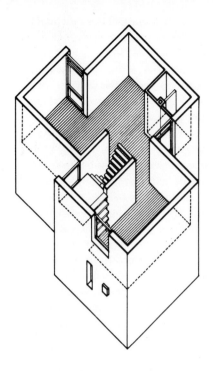

House in north London 1953

'The entire first floor is a single habitable area, and the ground floor, with the exception of the garage is considered as one space (kitchen-dining). On the top floor are three bedrooms. The principal sources of daylight (three vertical windows the full height of the building) give an unequal distribution of light to the interior. The diagonal range of internal vision is 34ft across the living room floor.'

Architect and Building News, 7 January 1959

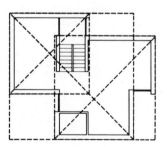

perpetually guarded about the personalities behind them.

Their lack of ingratiating qualities — colour, texture, atmosphere, anecdote — does not mean that they do not please, however, but that their pleasures are more akin to the mathematical elegance of some kinds of abstract art. Or to the kind of expository mechanical cut-away drawings of complex machinery to which Stirling and myself and the rest of our generation were heavily exposed during World War II. Those instruction manual drawings, intended to make it possible to strip, reassemble and, above all, *understand,* sophisticated and enigmatic items of machinery, were not necessarily elegant but they had to be clear at all costs. A good Stirling drawing is both elegant and clear. In the sections through the teaching wing of Olivetti Haslemere, for instance, the clarity of the relations of part to part (such as the pipe runs in the wall) and the deft wiriness of the line combine in an image that gladdens the mind as well as the eye.

It is a kind of drawn architectural image which is regrettably rare at the present time, when too much architectural draughtsmanship seems merely intent on blowing the minds of prospective clients, winning the favour of miniscule egg-head coteries in New York or London, or cleaning up the annual project-awards of trendy monthlies. For all their reticences about their author, and ambiguities about their function, a Stirling drawing is lucid in itself and explicit in its content. Appropriately enough, they are drawn always on tracing stock, and the light comes through them, much as the mind passes through and illuminates their intellectual transparency.

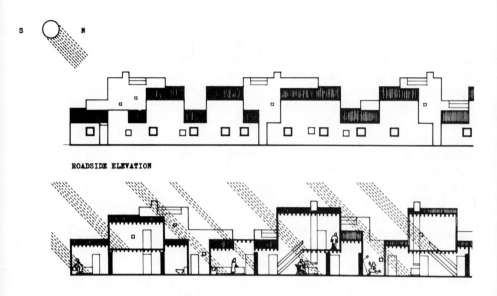

S ⊙ **N**

ROADSIDE ELEVATION

Village project (Team X) 1955

'While working in offices I did a project for Team X that was a reaction to driving through country villages and finding at the other end perhaps half a dozen houses tacked on by the Local Authority, usually semi-d's, unsympathetic to the scale and materials of the village. One had to propose a system appropriate to the size and formation of the English village and, therefore, it had to continue the linear street pattern. In principle it was a strip of three structural walls making two internal bays of different width.

From the outer walls spanned a lean-to roof, and walls and roof were to be made of any material, according to locality.'

An architect's approach to architecture, RIBA Journal, May 1965

15

Stirling on drawing
(In response to R. Banham's introduction)

(1) A drawing has to be designed. (viewpoint critical). Elimination of information is the crux and is achieved through a series of design decisions, often taken quickly in sequence; sometimes taking a lot of deliberation (more likely to be the less successful drawing). What is left on the image is the minimum required to convey the maximum information with the greatest clarity — related to how we 'understand' the building as distinct from the way it might in reality look (with colour, texture, 3D etc.). To do with our 'understanding' not particularly intended as pictorial. The axonometric drawings are very rarely shown to clients and are not used for presenting the building design to committees. This 'presentation' function is often done via models, i.e. Cambridge, Queens. The models are somewhat abstract, though they show form correctly and also the primary solid/skin/void relationships, but not materials colour texture etc.

(2) Drawings (axos) of assemblage type buildings (i.e. St Andrews, Runcorn) always show incomplete buildings but make explicit the assemblage process. Therefore an image of assemblage and not a building entity. In this sense I think axos for buildings like St Andrews, Olivetti are very suitable.

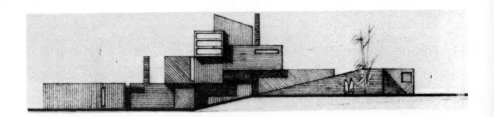

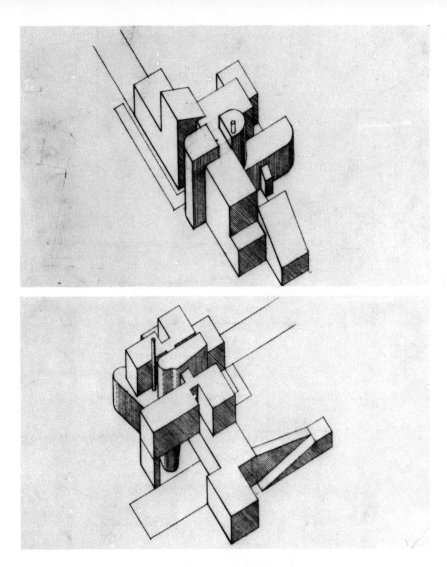

House studies 1956

'These are a series of academic exercises which were undertaken when the partnership was first formed to establish a working method.

It was considered desirable to express separately the existence of each functioning space within the terms of the main discipline and the results tended to be cluster assemblies. We decided that a more spontaneous, less intellectual use of materials, which directly solved each problem as it occurred, was likely to result in a greater vitality. Thus the fabric might be an amalgam of different materials each chosen for an immediate specific purpose.'

The work of Stirling and Gowan, Architect and Building News, 7 January 1959

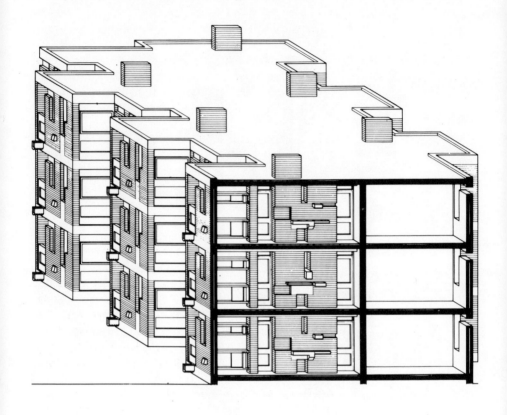

Flats at Ham Common, Richmond 1955/58

'There is probably more protest than is needed for the simple provision of a few flats. This is of course natural in an early commission, but for all that the attitude is far too common amongst this generation of designers.'

N. Pevsner, The Buildings of England: Surrey

FROM GARCHES TO JAOUL

Le Corbusier as domestic architect in 1927 and 1953

James Stirling

Originally published in the
Architectural Review,
September 1955

Villa Garches, recently reoccupied, and the two houses for Mr Jaoul and his son, now nearing completion, are possibly the most significant buildings by Le Corbusier to be seen in Paris to-day, for they represent the extremes of his vocabulary: the former, rational, urbane, programmatic, the latter, personal and anti-mechanistic. If style is the crystallization of an attitude, then these buildings, so different even at the most superficial level of comparison, may, on examination, reveal something of a philosophical change of attitude on the part of their author.

Garches, built at the culmination of Cubism and canonizing the theories in *Towards a new architecture.* has since its inception been a standard by which Le Corbusier's genuis is measured against that of the other great architects of this century. Inhabited, again by Americans, after fifteen years' splendid isolation, it has been painted in a manner more 'de Stijl' than the original: walls white inside and out, all structural members black and single planes of primary colour on areas of lesser consequence. It is never possible to see more than one coloured plane from any single viewpoint. On the principal facade, the underside of the entrance canopy is painted sky-blue as the underside of the slab over the terrace. Inside, one wall of the living area is painted yellow, etc.

As with the still deserted Poissy, the deterioration at Garches was only skin-deep; paint decay, broken glass and slight cracks in the rendering; there has been no deterioration to the structure nor any waterproofing failures. Though the landscape has thickened considerably to the rear of the house, trees have not yet grown close against the main facades; where this has happened, at La Roche, Cook and Pleinex, the balanced asymmetry of the elevations, as total compositions, has been grossly disfigured. The one instance among the

Paris buildings where trees are sympathetic is the Pavillon Suisse where they have grown the full height of the south elevation, significantly one of the most repetitive facades that Le Corbusier has produced. In more extreme examples of additive elevations, as in many American buildings, the presence of trees, naturalistic incidents, might almost be considered essential. The disembowelled machine parts of the Armée du Salut outbuildings have a similar juxtaposition to the neutral backdrop of the slab.

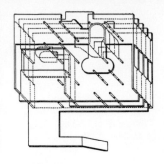

Villa Garches: axonometric view of basic structure

If Garches appears urban, sophisticated and essentially in keeping with 'l'esprit parisien', then the Jaoul houses seem primitive in character, recalling the Provencal farmhouse community; they seem out of tune with their Parisian environment. Their pyramidal massing is reminiscent of traditional Indian architecture and they were in fact designed after Le Corbusier's first visits to that country. Frequently accused of being 'internationalist', Le Corbusier is actually the most regional of architects. The difference between the cities of Paris and Marseilles is precisely the difference between the Pavillon Suisse and the Unité, and at Chandigarh the centre buildings are indebted to the history and traditions of a native Indian culture; even a project for the Palace of the Soviets makes considerable reference to Russian constructivism. Therefore, it is perhaps disturbing to encounter the Jaoul houses within half a mile of the Champs Elysées.

Assuming that the observer has become familiar with the architecture of Le Corbusier through the medium of the glossy books, then the first impression registered on arriving at the Jaoul houses is unique for they are of the scale and size expected, possibly because of the expressed floor beams. Usually, the scale is either greater or smaller than anticipated, that of Garches being unexpectedly heroic.

Differing from the point structure and therefore free plan of Garches, the structure of Jaoul is of load-bearing, brick cross-walls, cellular in planning by implication. It would, however, be a mistake to think of these buildings as models for cross-wall architecture as this aspect is

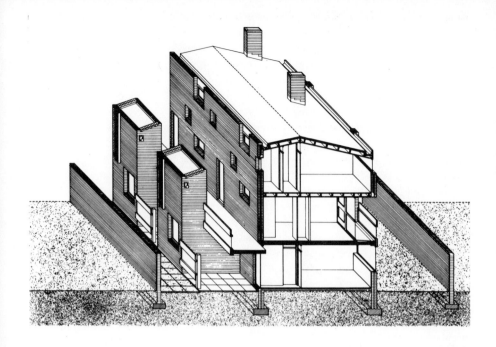

Preston infill housing 1957/59

'I have a notion that he suffers from a nostalgia of the slums. The celebrity he enjoys, his wealth, imprison him in a way of life in which he finds only constraint. I think he looks back to the freedom of his struggling youth, with its poverty and bitter privation with a longing which knows it can never be satisfied. To him the streets of southern London are the scene of frolic, gaiety and extravagant adventure. They have to him a reality which the well-kept avenue, bordered with trim houses, in which live the rich, can never possess. I can imagine him going into his own house, and wondering what on earth he is doing in this strange man's dwelling. I suspect the only home he can ever look upon as such is a second-floor back in the Kennington Road. One night I walked with him in Los Angeles and presently our steps took us into the poorest quarter of the city. There were sordid tenement houses and shabby, gaudy shops in which are sold the various goods that the poor buy from day to day. His face lit up and a bouyant tone came into his voice as he exclaimed "This is the real life isn't it? All the rest is just sham".'

Somerset Maughan on Charlie Chaplin, A writer's notebook.

21

visually subordinated to the massive, concrete, Catalan vaults occurring at each floor level. These vaults are to be covered with soil and grass to resist thermal expansion and the timber shutter-boards have been set to leave a carefully contrived pattern. Internally one-inch solid steel ties are positioned at approximately fifteen-foot centres to resist diagonal thrust into the brick walls. At the external centre point of these vaults, bird-nesting boxes are formed, and occasionally concrete rainwater heads are projected from the side-beams, though the pipes drop internally. Rising from the underground garage through to the top of each house are dog-leg stairs, cast in situ; they are a development from the Marseilles fire-escape stair, with the treads canti-levered either side of the vertical concrete slab. By English standards, the brickwork is poor, but then the wall is considered as a surface and not a pattern. Masonry, rubble, or, perhaps more rationally in view of the vault construction, mass concrete walls could be substituted without difference to the principle of design.

Perhaps the only factor that Garches and Jaoul have in common is the considerable influence of the site on both. All Le Corbusier's buildings tend to fall into one of two categories: those in which the peculiarities of the site are a paramount factor in conception — most notably the Armée du Salut — and those where the site is of little consequence, being subordinated to a preconception or archetype, e.g. the Unité. To some extent this may account for the lack of inevitability, sometimes felt with buildings of this latter category, most particularly the Pavillon Suisse where, except as an archetype per se, there seems little justification for raising the building above ground, there being no circulation or view through. If the entrance hall, approachable from any direction, had been under and not to the rear of the slab, the raising of the block would not appear so arbitrary. None the less, the town-planning ideas which generated this form retain their urgent validity.

The exact relationship and planning of the two Jaoul houses have been motivated by the nature of the site. The circulation is on two levels and of two kinds. Cars

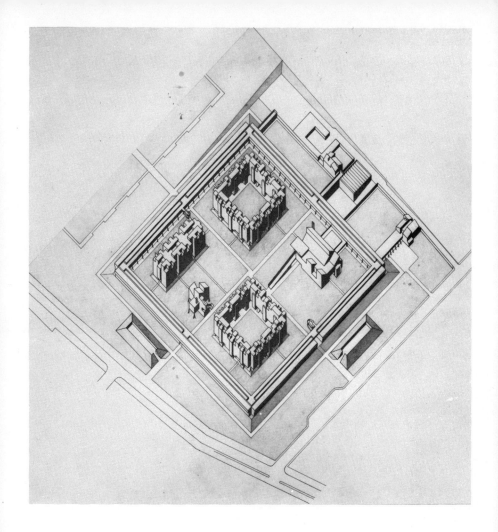

Churchill College 1958

The open, flat and almost rural character of the site indicated that in designing a group of buildings as a residential college it was important to create an internal environment, private, enclosed and protected.

From the report sent with the competition drawings.

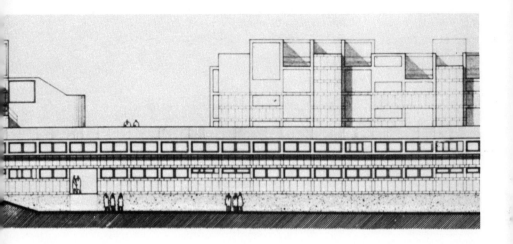

Churchill College 1958 (limited competition)

'A work of architecture is invariably an advertisement of a point of view. It is never pure form or pure function; nor can it be simply a mixture of both; but always, either forcibly or feebly, it involves an act of judgement. It is an attitude taken up with regard to society, history, change, the nature of pleasure, and other matters quite extraneous to either technique or taste. Thus, a work of architecture, while always an index to state of mind, may quite often be constructed as an illicit manifesto; and the typical work of modern architecture was until recently quite often to be interpreted in this way.'

C. Rowe, The Blenheim of the welfare state, The Cambridge Review, 31 October 1959

drive straight off the road into the garage, a large underground cavern from which separate stairs rise through to each house. Walking circulation is above this garage on what appears to be natural ground level but which is actually a made-up terrace on which the houses stand. This level is linked to the road by a ramp. The differentiation of circulation on superimposed levels and the free movement around the houses are reminiscent in another medium of the suspended routes into the Armée du Salut.

At Maison Jaoul the only entire elevation that can be seen from a single viewpoint is to the rear and has to be observed over the garden wall of the adjoining private property. Owing to the narrowness of the plot, all other facades have to be viewed either episodically through the trees or close up at an oblique angle. The solid-void relationship of the exterior does not appear to follow any easily apparent scheme. This is a development from Le Corbusier's earlier work where at La Roche the drawing board elevation also cannot be seen at right angles and the studied balance of window to wall is destroyed. This is due not only to the trees which have grown since but especially to the necessity of viewing the elevation at a sharp angle.

The hierarchic presentation of external elements occurs also in the work of Frank Lloyd Wright, where the most important feature is the corner, and this may account for much of the undergrowth against the facades proper. It may be argued that the only exterior which can maintain interest, as the eye moves at an equal distance around the corner, is the cage or box. The most notable example of this is the Lake Shore Apartments where it would be inappropriate to suggest a 'principal facade'. Poissy almost comes into the category of the box but only on three sides; the fourth, receiving no undercut, becomes a vertical plane differing from the dynamic horizontality of the others. At Garches there is no point in moving around the corner for there is a very definite axis and the side elevations are of little consequence, their window openings positioned functionally make no attempt to arrive at a formal composition. The site boundary lines, defined by tall, closely planted trees, are

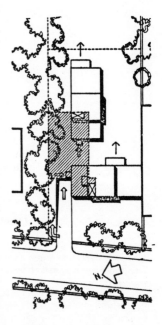

Maison Jaoul, rue de Longchamps, Neuilly-sur-Seine site plan

26

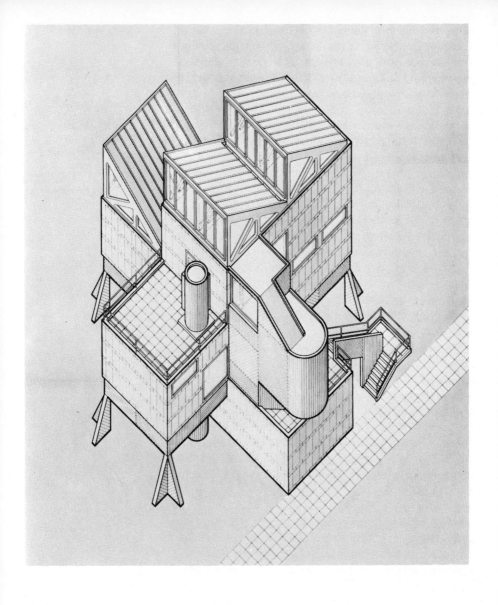

Churchill College 1958

The library building with dead book storage at ground level. The reading rooms and book stacks are at first and second floor levels. Roof trusses with clear-storey windows provide lighting to the interior of the reading spaces.

about six feet from each of these side elevations, making it almost impossible to see them. The long facades, on the contrary, may be seen head on from a considerable distance by the approaching visitor and their balanced asymmetry is masterfully exploited.

Internally, space departs radically from the structure; an explosion in terms of Cubist space is contained within the four peripheral walls which externally give little evidence of this phenomenon, contained except where it escapes and rushes out along the direction of the terrace, to be finally dissipated in the heavy landscape. However, space is not contrived for the sake of effect only, it invariably has a psychological as well as a functional context. For instance, on passing through the front door, the immediate double height and the presence of a stair indicate that the main floor is above. Similarly, the diagonal spatial stress across the first floor suggests the route through the house.

The main living areas are flooded with an even intensity of light, but, where accommodation and circulation are of lesser consequence, natural lighting becomes more restricted and as one moves through the house a continuous contrast in definitions is attained. 'The elements of architecture are light and shade, walls and space.' The natural light which penetrates to the interior of the Jaoul houses is consistently subdued and not dissimilar to that found inside many Frank Lloyd Wright buildings.

Eventually somebody will have to consider the numerous similarities between Le Corbusier and Wright, and their common differences from the work of Mies van der Rohe. For instance, the pattern of circulation, repetitive on all floors as in the Pavillon Suisse and many of Le Corbusier's larger buildings, becomes in some of his and Wright's domestic works a route so complex and involved, as at Pleinex, that it is with the greatest difficulty that the stranger finds his way out. To a lesser extent, this applies at Jaoul and again, similar to Wright, the spatial effects, though exciting, are unexpected, encountered suddenly on turning a corner or glimpsed on passing a slit in the wall. Where double height does

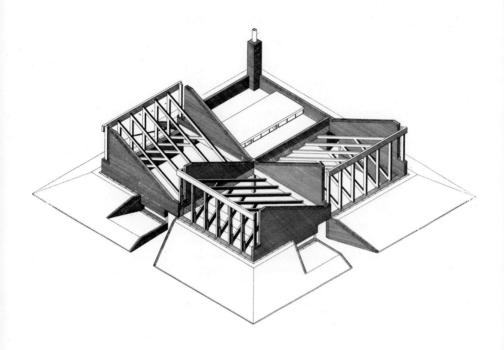

School Assembly Hall, Camberwell 1958/61

The plan is divided into quarters; two parts for the hall (sub-dividable) and one for the kitchen, and the remaining quarter for service rooms (stores, boiler house) which has a flat roof.

From the mid-point of the retaining walls, four RC beams span onto a single column at the centre of the plan. Over three of the quarters large timber roof trusses span from the retaining wall onto the RC beam and support the roof which tilts up to direct light into the interior.

From the report to committee.

occur in one of the living rooms it appears as a dead area, having no secondary use such as the vertical height of the Unité flats which lights and ventilates the bedroom. If the space inside Garches can be considered dynamic, then here it is static; there is certainly no question of being able to stand inside and comprehend at a glance the limits of the house, as at Garches.

Implicit in the structural system, rooms tend to be small boxes with the living areas more generous. The internal finishes have a greater variety and richness of surface than at Garches, where, with the exception of the floor, the materials, though not the form, of the walls and ceilings are neutralised. Inside Jaoul, concrete is left shutter-marked, walls are plastered or brick fair-faced, floors are tiled and there is a considerable variety and quantity of timber and, most significantly, the ceiling or underside of the vaults is frequently finished in a dark clay tile which cannot be expected to amplify 'the magnificent play of light on form'. The 'fourth wall' — the incorporation of shelving and opaque materials into the window opening — is symptomatic of Le Corbusier's recent attitude to surface depth. Windows are no longer to be looked through but looked at. The eye finding interest in every part of the surface impasto, does not, as at Garches, seek relief from the hard textureless finish by examining the contours and form of the plane.

Maison Jaoul is no doubt dimensioned according to 'Le Modulor', a development from the application of the golden section by regulating lines as at Garches, where it is possible to read off the inter-relations of squares and sections as the eye traverses the facade and where, internally, every element is positioned according to an exact geometrical hierarchy. In fact, Garches must be considered the masterpiece of Neo-Palladianism in modern architecture, conceived in plan, section, elevation from two proportions which, owing to their particular inter-relationship, achieve an organic or harmonic whole as distinct from an additive total. The variety of dimensions available from 'Le Modulor' are considerable and as Bodiansky (The structural engineer for the Marseilles Unite) has said 'there is always a figure near at hand to adjust to'. This considerable flexibility

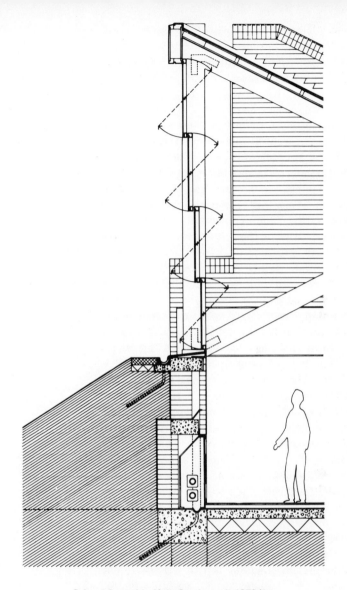

School Assembly Hall, Camberwell 1958/61

The immediate neighbourhood is very poor and the adjoining buildings are of a great variety of types and heights, and in this situation of architectural chaos and crowded slums we consider it necessary to compact the building and make an island of open space and green lawns, and the new building is therefore integrated into the landscape by engulfing grass banks. Internally this forms a continuous retaining wall which is also useful for gymnastics and playing ball games against. Above this wall are high level studio type windows.

From the report to committee.

31

may create a visually non-apparent geometry, as at Jaoul, but here the restrictions of the site already mentioned must be remembered when considering whether this is a valid criticism.

Garches is an excellent example of Le Corbusier's particular interpretation of the machine aesthetic. The body of the house, built by quite conventional methods for its time, has skin-walls of concrete block rendered to a monolithic, poured or sprayed effect; an aesthetic for a structural system not yet in being. Yet while Garches is not the product of any high-powered mechanisation, the whole spirit of the building expresses the essence of machine power. To be on the first floor is to witness the Mumfordian end product of twentieth-century technology, 'the silent, staffless power-house'. The incorporation of rail-road and steamship fabrication is decidedly technocrat and the integration of architecture to specialist requirements extremely considered as the boiler-house disposed like an industrial engine-room or the timber-strip flooring obviously laid by ship's carpenters. The type of detailing in synthetic materials here and at the Armée du Salut is almost the last of the steam-age period; crude maybe, it is nevertheless powerful. After this date, the number of synthetic materials per building increases, and, as at the Pavillon Suisse, the detailing becomes more refined but somehow less memorable. There is no reference to any aspect of the machine at Jaoul either in construction or aesthetic. These houses, total cost £30,000, are being built by Algerian labourers equipped with ladders, hammers and nails, and with the exception of glass no synthetic materials are being used; technologically, they make no advance on medieval building. The timber window-wall units may be prefabricated but as with technology one suspects that prefabrication must begin with the structure.

To imply that these houses will be anything less than magnificent art would be incorrect. Their sheer plastic virtuosity is beyond emulation. Nevertheless, on analysis, it is disturbing to find little reference to the rational principles which are the basis of the modern movement, and it is difficult to avoid assessing these

Selwyn College 1959

'The new building also acted as a wall, maintaining the privacy of a fine garden for members of the College. All rooms focussed with a view across the garden and the existing College. The glass screen was really an enormous window faceting in and out approximately indicating on the exterior the scale of the students rooms and sets; and College members walking in the grounds would have seen reflected in the glass a shattered Cubist image of the trees in the garden.'

An architect's approach to architecture, RIBA Journal, May 1965

buildings except in terms of 'art for art's sake'. More so than any other architect of this century, Le Corbusier's buildings present a continuous architectural development which, however, has not recently been supplemented by programmatic theory.

As homes the Jaoul houses are almost cosy and could be inhabited by any civilised family, urban or rural. They are built by and intended for the status quo. Conversely, it is difficult to imagine Garches being lived in spontaneously except by such as the Sitwells, with never less than half a dozen brilliant, and permanent, guests. Utopian, it anticipates, and participates in, the progress of twentieth-century emancipation. A monument, not to an age which is dead, but to a way of life which has not generally arrived, and a continuous reminder of the quality to which all architects must aspire if modern architecture is to retain its vitality.

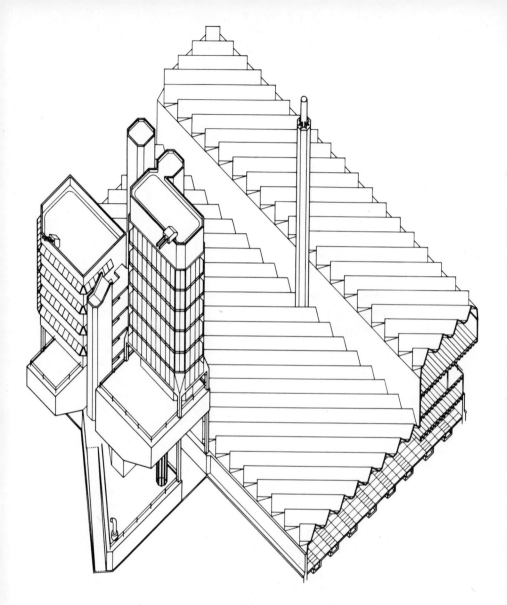

Leicester University Engineering Building 1959/63

'All built form has weight and properties of stability or instability dependant on shape and it is necessary to make a grouping of masses which is inherently stable. In the Engineering Building, the weight of the towers above counterbalances the overhang of the lecture theatres under, or to say it another way, the extent of the cantilever of the lecture theatres is dictated by the amount of weight over; if you removed the top floor the building would overturn. No doubt there is a certain architectural quality inherent in the composition of stable masses particularly when they are asymmetrical.'

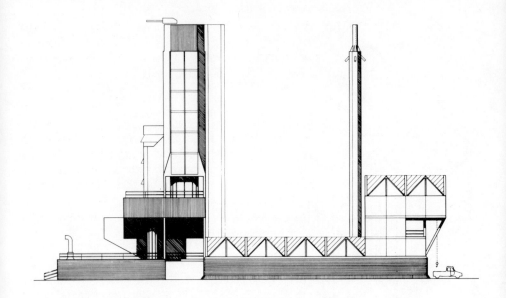

Leicester University Engineering Building 1959/63

'. . . lecture theatres jutting out. These are of exposed concrete; the rest is faced with blue engineering bricks . . .'

N. Pevsner, The anti-pioneers, The Listener, 5 January 1967

'The brickwork is red not blue. Both lecture theatres (as elsewhere) are entirely covered by red tiles, they are not of exposed concrete.'

JS letter, The Listener, 12 January 1967

It is clear that when Professor Pevsner approaches a building which he THINKS he should not like — he closes his eyes. JS.

ANTI-STRUCTURE

A slide talk given by James Stirling at Bologna University during a Symposium (November 1966) to mark the retirement of Professor Giovanni Michelucci from the School of Architecture.

I understand the subject for discussion at this Symposium is the relevance of structure in architecture. This is not a very appropriate subject for me as I have a rather ad hoc and expedient attitude to structure particularly as a design element and I usually manage to prevent it from intruding in the architectural solution. I'm more concerned with sociological, environmental, and organisational problems which I regard as being more important in the evolution of a design.

I suspect I'm considered by many English architects (and some of the architectural press) as a somewhat irrational designer. (We have inherited the Bauhaus mentality just as America has inherited the Beaux Arts.) However, I would argue that our buildings usually evolve from a broad but complex understanding of logic. Logic is many faceted and its properties are normally not the same for every building. Each project has its own importance hierarchy, sometimes indicated by the client's brief and always determined by the sensibility of the architect. I would like to comment on some factors which have influenced our work, and as you may be familiar with these projects, I will try to keep to aspects which have not been described previously.

In the design for a children's home in South London we thought social considerations should have priority. The children who grow up in these homes are either orphans or have been taken from families where the parents cannot look after them. We wanted the new buildings to over-compensate for the lack of a real 'home'. Small in size, they are almost a caricature of the domestic house and they have the small scale of doll's houses and children's toys. The more costly decision to make two buildings instead of one was in order to reduce the size of the 'family' to about fifteen children per house instead of thirty as it would have been in a single building. We thought it important not to make the scheme institutional. Each house is looked after by a married couple who really become foster parents and, like an ordinary house, the children's bedrooms are on the upper floor. Seen from outside, each room steps back, causing the facade to recede and articulate the bedrooms, indicating them as the important spaces within the building. Children playing in the gardens are able to identify with their own particular room.

The expression (articulation) of the important accommodation is something we have always been concerned with and in our first project — the flats at Ham Common — the entity of the dwellings was indicated by the forward and backward movement of the facade. These flats were built in the garden of a Georgian house and we made the new buildings of similar materials and kept to the same height. Modern buildings need not necessarily be visually disruptive to adjoining old buildings.

In the re-housing scheme at Preston, the front door of each dwelling is onto an elevated footpath and opposite this door is a storage outhouse. This outhouse identifies the position of the dwelling within the terrace and, although the density is twice the existing, the new buildings are of similar height and materials to the houses in the adjoining nineteenth century streets. I have doubts about the accepted solution for re-building slum areas in the form of slabs or towers, which are physically disruptive to a neighbourhood and probably create an inferior social community. Lifts, in their present form, are a crude and anti-social way of approaching one's home.

Leicester University Engineering Building 1959/63

This sketch is one of several which were used to indicate to the patent glazing specialist the glass/mullion junctions prior to the preparation of preliminary shop drawings.

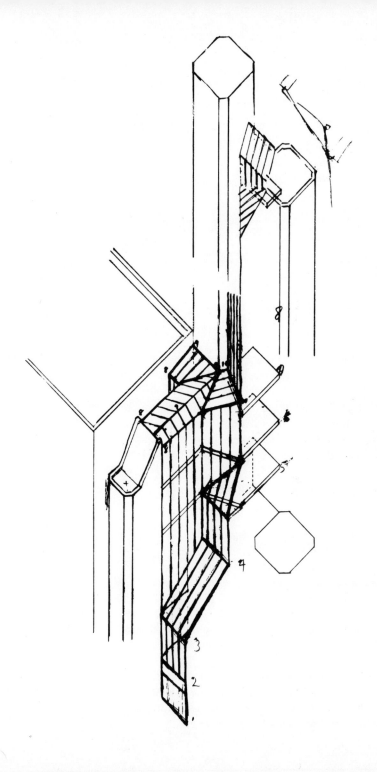

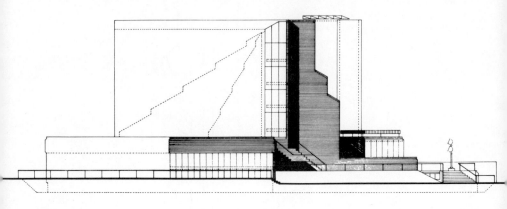

Probably as a country we spend less per square foot on our buildings than most countries of Western Europe and all the projects I have worked on are of low cost. With the smaller buildings, we have resorted to our surviving craft tradition of bricklaying. This slow hand-made process does, of course, pose philosophical problems in the middle of the twentieth century. However, if it is still a viable economic/labour method for our building industry, then it is surely realistic for us to use it.

After six or seven years designing very articulated buildings, we decided, in the old peoples' home at Blackheath, to do the opposite. Here, none of the accommodation is expressed; all rooms are concealed behind a screen of structural brick walls which wrap around an internal garden. Perhaps this is our only perverse building, and maybe, it has some resemblance to style 'à la liberté', popular here some time back.

All these projects were domestic in function and concerned with maintaining the status quo in relation to their environs; and they are essentially conventional in their re-statement of traditional internal use.

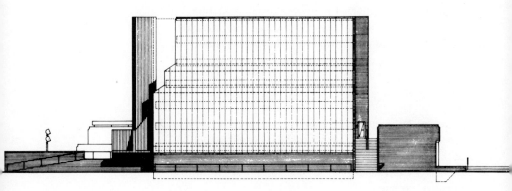

Cambridge University History Building 1964/67

'... but visually alas part of the Faculty of Arts buildings. Perhaps, if Sir Hugh Casson had not been so playful, James Stirling might not have been so rude. People in the last ten years have spoken about anti-art. Here — and only here at Cambridge — is anti-architecture. Here is an intelligent, resourceful architect making it his busines to design a building which fulfils all the functional demands and yet is actively ugly — not ugly in the vociferous way of the brutalists, but ugly more basically, by avoiding anything that might attract.'

N. Pevsner, The Buildings of England: Cambridgeshire.

'My guess is that he (JS) starts with the programme and thinks very hard about it and turns it over and over in his mind until the programme becomes itself a kind of hieroglyph, a sort of shape which has no very obvious and evident relationship to the function of the building, but does in fact satisfy those functions and becomes something rather strange and original. Anyway, that for me is why the building fascinates me I think more than any other very recent building.'

J. Summerson, Building Design, 4 June 1976

With the engineering building for Leicester University we had to build a new institution of a scientific/educational type. The tower at the front contains the fixed non-expanding accommodation and is intended to be a grouping of identifiable volumes of accommodation, i.e. vertical shafts which are for lifts and staircases, wedge-shaped volumes which are lecture theatres, etc. The back of the building is considered as a shed, within which there can be continuous re-equipping and adjustment of spaces.

The total building should read as a conjunction of fixed, specific activities and of a variable changing situation, both reflecting the educational curriculum. The organisational circumstance which was different from our previous experience is the fact that 200 to 300 students move rapidly through the circulation in a stop/go process several times a day, changing classes; this movement factor largely influenced the planning solution and the building section. The vertical circulation, which includes lay-bys adjacent to the lift and staircase shafts, is the skeleton onto which various rooms are hung and the circulation routes are the only consistent visual element running through the building, in comparison to the differing visual characteristics of specific rooms. We have not attempted to carry through an 'interior design' idiom and the function of a room has been the sole determinate of its internal appearance. This is different from some contemporary buildings, for instance the Yale School of Architecture which contains a lecture theatre, staff rooms, library, guest suite etc. as well as studios and all are treated in a similar interior aesthetic-ribbed concrete (brought in from the exterior). The same materials and surfaces are used throughout, inside and out, which I would have thought

Cambridge University History Building 1964/67

The History building is also intended to be read as a grouping of identifiable elements, i.e. lift and staircase shafts and most obviously the large tent shaped roof indicating the library reading room below, the largest internal space.

. . . the room shapes are stacked to become the total building form and it is possible to see that the smaller rooms are on the top floors, increasing to larger and largest rooms at the lower levels.'

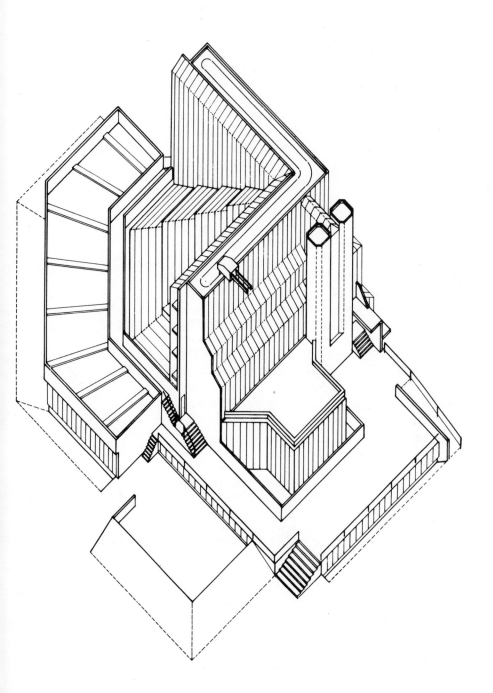

incompatible and illogical for such divergent activities. In the engineering building each type of room has its own interior aesthetic and, in a similar way, the structural support changes for different parts of the building — the type of construction chosen being the most appropriate to the dimensions and activity of a particular space, i.e. industrial spaceframe roof across the workshops; disconnected acoustic shell within an R.C. insitu box for the lecture theatres; R.C. diagrid spanning between peripheral columns over the research labs. There are as many structural systems as there are major differences in function and the choice of the type of structure was a later decision in the design evolution.

There is however, a more important aspect to structure than the selection of constructional systems and this relates to the initial concept of the building mass.

All built form has weight and properties of stability or instability dependant on shape and it is necessary to make a grouping of masses which is inherently stable. In the engineering building, the weight of the towers above counterbalances the overhang of the lecture theatres under, or to say it another way, the extent of the cantilever of the lecture theatres is dictated by the amount of weight over; if you removed the top floor the building would overturn. No doubt there is a certain

Cambridge University History Building 1964/67

The entrance/exit to the reading room opens directly into a control and enquiry area where the catalogues are housed; beyond and 4ft below this level is the reading room. The book stack is on two levels and the shelving units fan radially on sight lines from the control desk, which thus has total supervision of the reading room and book stack. The control desk is also a console from which heating, lighting and ventilation is adjusted. The extract machines at the top of the glazed roof are also controlled from this desk. . . . the under skin of glazing is translucent, producing shadowless natural light on the reading room tables . . . The 'brief' suggests that close contact between the reading room and the other accommodation is essential and the arrangement of corridors as galleries around the reading room is a principal factor of the planning.

From the report submitted with the competition drawings.

The model was made in the office and was used for studying the space and daylighting of the reading room; it was not used for presentation to the Building Committee.

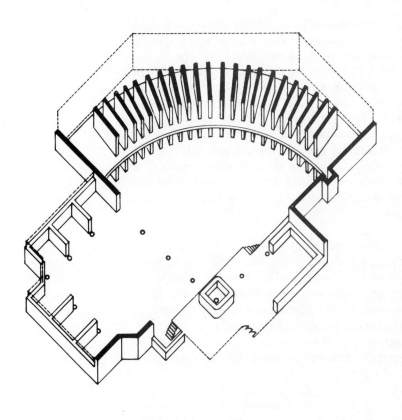

architectural quality inherent in the composition of stable masses particularly when they are a-symmetrical.

The small elements of a building should, wherever possible, be multi-functioning, a more subtle requirement than the simplistic relationship of one to one elements; for instance, the sloping underside to the large lecture theatre is also the canopy over the entrance porch. At a smaller scale, the beams normally at the ceiling are on the floor of the offices and they are made as upstand beams which are simultaneously a window seat, a horizontal duct for services and a fire barrier between floors, as well as being structural beams. The shafts which contains the lifts and staircases are the vertical service ducts as well as being structural buttresses.

The diagonal displacement of the roof over the workshops was necessary to obtain north lighting but it also allowed a superimposition of two geometries, the normal (right angular) and the distorted (at 45°) like a Cubist image. There is liberation and a greater number of planning choices available when more than one geometry is integrated into the design. It has also been said that axonometric drawing technique has influenced the design of this building.

The History Faculty for Cambridge University is also intended to be read as a grouping of identifiable elements, i.e. lift and staircase shafts and most obviously the large tent shaped roof indicating the library reading room below, the largest internal space.

A vast amount of modern architecture is banal, partly through the easy acceptance of compressing room accommodations into simple overall building forms. We usually try to retain the ideal shape of a room and avoid distorting it to fit a structural module or a preconceived building shape. In the History Faculty the room shapes are stacked to become the total building form and it is possible to see that the smaller rooms are on the top floors, increasing to larger and largest rooms at the lower levels.

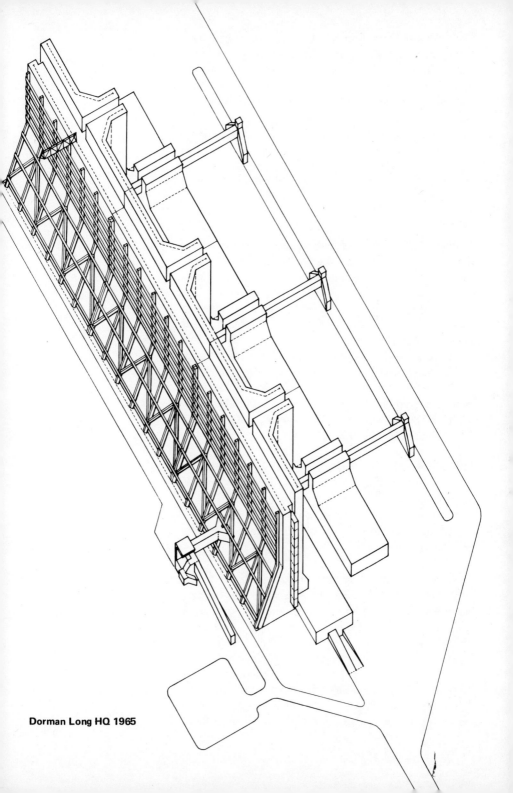

Dorman Long HQ 1965

The open steel truss roof which leans across the reading room allows daylight to filter into the library and, at the upper levels, it also allows light through into the circulation corridors. This roof is also a technical element, a controlled climate cushion containing heaters, ventilation louvres, fan extracts, lights, etc. automatically adjusting to the outside climate to maintain a constant atmosphere within. The thrust from this 'lean-to-roof' is stabilised by the buttressing effect of the 'L' shaped block and the total building mass is a resolvement of various structural forces.

The exterior is of similar materials to the engineering building — glass, tiles, etc. — hard, brittle and reflective surfaces appropriate to the outside climate. These materials are not brought into the interior and the walls of the library, etc. are lined with acoustic finishes. The visual aesthetic inside is, if anything, more like that of a television studio. The corridors are thought of as galleries running around the upper spaces of the reading room, they are glazed for sound and are the primary circulation system. The students moving about the building are visually in contact with the library, the most important working element of the Faculty. This interrelationship was developed from an implication in the Faculty's brief for the new building.

The next projects are significantly different as both have an external appearance of expressed structure. This is not however a rejection of our previous work; it is just that these buildings have extraordinary circumstances which made considerations of structure top of the importance hierarchy.

The new buildings for St Andrews University are in the north of Scotland where there is no local building material (not even bricks) or workmen (who have all come south). The problem was how to erect a battery of student residences as a continuous building process over a period of six or seven years. The only method which seemed possible was to design a kit of precast concrete elements to be manufactured elsewhere. These are taken to the site where they are lifted directly off lorries by mobile cranes and placed onto the building without

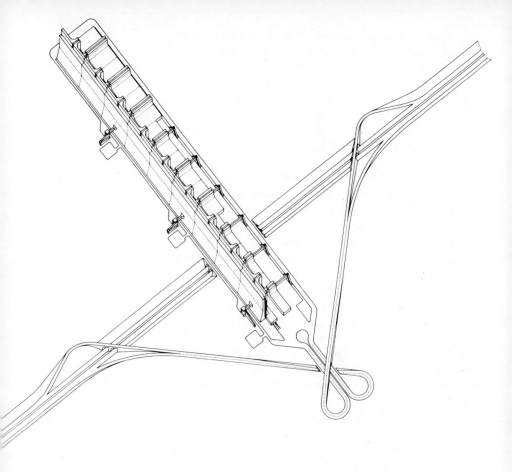

Dorman Long HQ 1965

The accommodation includes many small offices and these are positioned in the upper floors. The larger (i.e. computer centre) and more public elements (i.e. canteen, dining rooms, cinema, drawing offices etc) are located on the lower floors and this accounts for the thickening of the building section towards the ground and the outward splay of the building front.

From the report to committee.

'The English steel industry is about to be nationalised and there are doubts as to the future of this project, though as the Dorman Long building could be expanded to become the headquarters of a north east steel group, the building might grow to be three times longer. It would then be lying across the intended siting of a new motorway which the local authority are reluctant to move. However the road could go straight through the building, or dip down under and the building would then also be a bridge.'

Anti-Structure, Zodiac No. 18

49

touching ground. The factory is in Edinburgh, about eighty miles south of St Andrews. Each building is assembled from a range of precast wall and floor units and there are about thirtytwo different moulds which will be re-used for the later buildings. The first building is expensive but the cost should be more economical with the later residences and the overall cost could be similar to that of traditional buildings.

There are 250 students in each residence (both sexes) and the students' bedrooms are positioned in the fingers, which are pointed towards a magnificent view of the North Sea and the Scottish mountains. The non-repetitive accommodation (i.e. dining hall, games rooms, etc.) is located in the web where the fingers join. There is a glazed promenade level about halfway up the building and, from this, internal staircases give access up or down to the students' rooms. This promenade is the main artery of circulation and is intended to be the major element of sociability. Off the promenade and adjacent to the staircases are lay-bys containing seats and vending machines. In these areas it is hoped that much of the social life in the residence will take place and, in using the promenade on route to their rooms, every student will inevitably come into contact with everyone else. On the floors above and below the promenade the staircases give onto short, unpleasant corridors (deliberately narrow and under-lit) to the students' rooms. Sometimes it is necessary to design unpleasant spaces in order to increase the usage of areas where activity is intended. There was an elementary problem of identity inside the internal staircases — at what level does the promenade occur? — how to know when to get out. To help visually locate, large circular holes were cut into the walls of the staircases at promenade level; not an inside/outside window in the normal sense, it is therefore different from the rectangular windows used elsewhere. The sexes change with each staircase though I don't think the University realise that, as fire exits were required onto the roof, it should be possible for the students to cross over at night unseen. The student's private room is obviously the most important accommodation in the building and every room has a window angled like an eye towards the view. This angling which

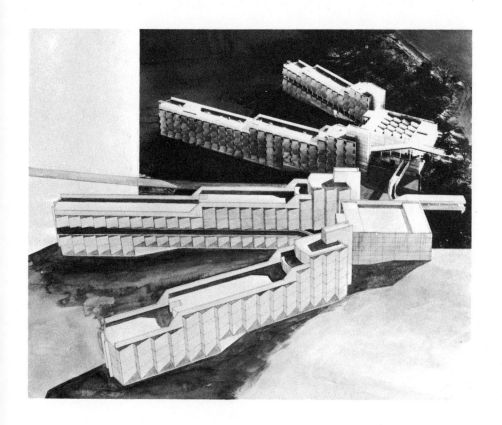

Residential expansion: St Andrews University 1964/68

The site is about one mile from the town and the view is magnificent across mountains and the North Sea. All rooms in the residences have windows orientated to this prospect. The main approach from the town is by a footpath which runs along the ridge and entry into each of the halls is down an enclosed staircase.

Note: the collage above incorporates an aerial photograph of the completed first building.

is a displacement of the room articulates its position on the facade and therefore, even with a very structurally motivated scheme, we have maintained as fundamental the expression of the most important accommodation.

If the site at St Andrews is idyllic, then the site for the Dorman Long building must be considered satanic; positioned at the end of the steel mills and surrounded by the symbols of heavy industry — slag mountains, cooling towers, flaming chimneys, etc. Dorman Long are England's largest producers of rolled steel columns and beams and they have a long history of civil engineering from Sydney Harbour Bridge to radio telescopes. They asked for the building to be of steel construction and for it to be an exposition of their standard products. Not only had the building to be made of steel, it had to be seen to be made of steel. This was a commercial requirement and we accepted it, partly as we think the future will see a considerable development in the steel medium for building (as well as assemblage methods of erection — i.e. St Andrews). Inevitably their request meant that the appearance of a structural system would dominate the architectural solution.

The headquarters office building is fourteen storeys high, and almost 1,000 feet long. The accommodation includes many small rooms — secretaries, managers, directors etc. and areas of large spaces — drawing offices, open plan offices, canteen, library, computer centre etc, amongst others. The larger spaces are on the lower floors and this accounts for the thickening of the building section towards the ground, indicated by the splayed front. The thrust created by this splay is counter-balanced by the shafts of vertical circulation pulled out behind which act as buttresses stabilising the total building form.

The English steel industry is about to be nationalised and there are doubts as to the future of this project, though as the Dorman Long building could be expanded to become the headquarters of a north east steel group, the building might grow to be three times longer. It would then be lying across the intended siting of a new motorway which the local authority are reluctant to

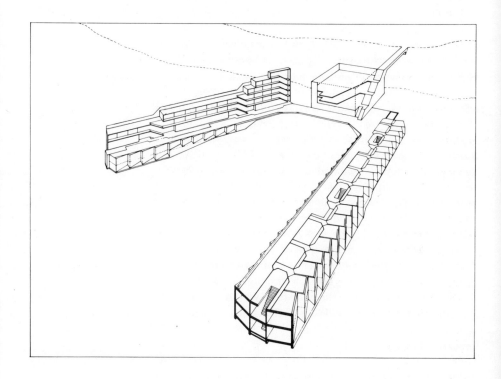

Residential expansion: St Andrews University 1964/68

'Recently, Stirling has extended his design method into prefabricated concrete and plastic. The St Andrews residence for university students makes use of concrete load bearing walls which delineate each student's room and set up interesting zig-zag patterns. But the organisational clarity remains the same. This scheme is organised around a circulation "deck" midway up the building which unifies the whole scheme and acts as a place of meeting, sort of a linear agora which overlooks the social activities outside. Students watch each other and are on display as they walk around the deck. Concerts, soccer, picnics, sunbathing take place in the landscaped area between the two legs of the building.'

C. Jencks, Environmental communications, Venice, California.

move. However, the road could go straight through the building, or dip down under (Orly Airport) and the building would then also be a bridge.

An interesting situation arose when a particular design of the external grid of columns and beams was being considered by the structural engineers. It transpired that there was a choice of about six alternatives for this structural mesh, all using approximately the same weight of steel and all of similar cost, i.e. it could be all diagonally braced, or it could have horizontal stiffener beams at every floor level, etc. The choice of a particular structural appearance was therefore arbitrary, reinforcing my opinion that a design, which is primarily dependant on expression of structure is likely to be superficial. To resolve this problem we made an architectural decision and kept the horizontal wind stiffener beams adjacent to each floor on the upper part of the building, but on the splayed front we omitted them at every other level, replacing them with diagonal struts to maintain the strength of structural mesh. The scale of the structural grid therefore relates to the building section and graphically indicates the smaller accommodation at the top and the larger accommodation below.

In England I find that, when making a presentation to the client, we must never talk about aesthetics and explanations should always be in terms of common sense, function and logic. If you mentioned the word 'beauty' their hair might stand on end and you could lose the commission. Perhaps this philistine attitude is, in some ways, beneficial as it probably means that a design can never be too far removed from common sense and logic.

The structural content in architecture is likely to increase as traditional methods of construction decline and new buildings get larger and more complicated. However, I think it will be ever more necessary for architects not to rely merely on the expression of techniques for the architectural solution. Humanistic considerations must remain the primary logic from which a design evolves.

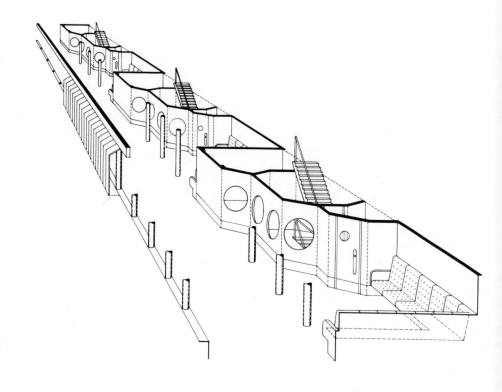

Residential expansion: St Andrews University 1964/68

'The promenade is the only route to the other student stacks and to the world outside and three large portholes have been slotted into the internal wall to help students realise they have reached this important level. The promenade has indented lay-bys fitted with bench seats and Stirling visualised this modern cloister and viewing gallery as a meeting area.'

Judy Hillman, The Observer colour supplement, 31 May 1970

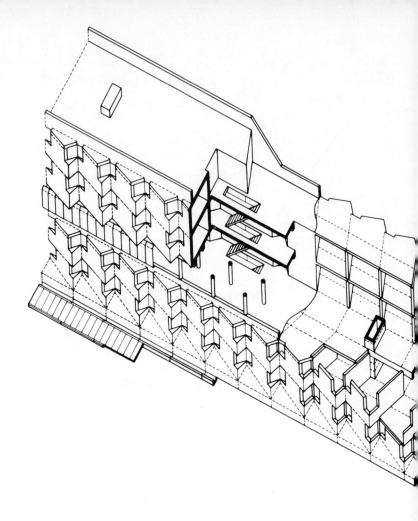

Residential expansion: St Andrews University 1964/68

The only method which seemed possible was to design a kit of precast concrete elements to be manufactured elsewhere. These are taken to 'the site where they are lifted directly off lorries oy mobile cranes and placed onto the building without touching ground. The factory is in Edinburgh, about eighty miles south of St Andrews. Each building is assembled from a range of precast wall and floor units and there are about thirty-two different moulds which will be re-used for the later buildings.

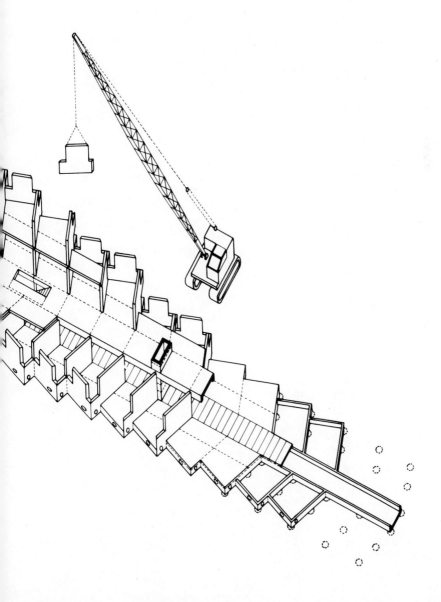

Projects

James Stirling	1950	Thesis
	50	Honan Competition (limited competition)
	51	Core and Crosswall House
	51	Stiff dom-ino housing
	51	ICA furniture
	52	Poole Technical College (national competition)
	53	Sheffield University (national competition with A. Cordingley)
	53	House in north London
	54	Woolton House
	55	Village project (Team x)

James Stirling and	55/58	Ham Common flats
James Gowan	56/58	Isle of Wight house
	56	House studies
	56	House in the Chilterns
	57	Three houses for B. Mavrolean family (limited competition)
	57/59	House conversion Kensington
	57	Expandable house
	57/59	Preston infill housing (tender cost competition)
	58	Steel mill cladding
	58	Churchill College (limited competition)
	58/61	School Assembly Hall, Camberwell
	59	Selwyn College
	59/63	Leicester University Engineering Building
	60/64	Old peoples home
	60/64	Childrens home

James Stirling	64/67	Cambridge University History Building (limited competition)
	64/68	Flats at Camden Town
	64/68	Residential expansion: St Andrews University
	65	Dorman Long HQ
	66/71	Queens College, Oxford
	67/76	Runcorn New Town, housing
	68	Redevelopment study, New York, USA (with A. Baker)
	69/76	Lima, Peru: Low cost housing (limited competition)
	69/72	Olivetti Training School, Haslemere
	69	Siemens AG, Munich (limited competition)
	70	Derby Town Centre (limited competition)

James Stirling and	71	Olivetti HQ, Milton Keynes
Michael Wilford	71	Arts Centre, St Andrews University
	72/77	Southgate (2) Housing, Runcorn
	75	Museum for Northrhine Westphalia, Dusseldorf (invited competitor)
	75	Wallraf-Richartz Museum, Cologne (invited competitor)
	76—	Meineke Strasse, Berlin
	76—	Government Centre, Doha (limited competition)
	76—	Regional Centre for Tuscany (national competition with Castore, Malanima, Rizzi)
	77—	Administration Centre, Wilaya De Skikda, Algeria
	77—	Museum of Science and Technology, Iran
	77—	UNEP. HQ. Nairobi (with G.De Carlo and Mutiso Menezes)
	77	Revisions to the Nolli Plan for Rome
	77—	Dresdner Bank, Marburg, Germany
	77—	Extension of The National Art Gallery, Stuttgart (limited competition)

First date is year of design
Second date is year of building completion

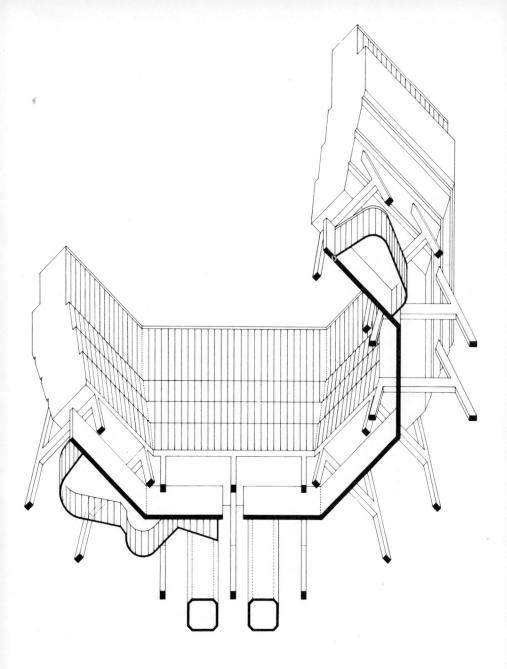

Queens College, Oxford 1966/71

Articles by JS

From Garches to Jaoul	Architectural Review, September 1955
Ronchamp and the crises of nationalism	Architectural Review, March 1956
This is tomorrow	Exhibition Catalogue, 1956
Regionalism and modern architecture	Architects Year Book No. 8, 1957
A personal view of the present situation	Architectural Design, June 1958
Packaged deal and prefabrication	Design, March 1959
The functional tradition and expression	Perspecta No. 6, Yale, USA, 1959 Cuadernos, Suma Nueva Vision, Buenos Aires, 1970
Architects' approach to architecture	RIBA Journal, May 1965 Kentiko Bunka, Japan, January 1967 Zodiac No. 16, Italy, 1967 Cuadernos, Suma Nueva Vision, Buenos Aires, 1970
Conversations with students	Perspecta No. 12 Yale, USA, 1967 Cuadernos, Suma Nueva Vision, Buenos Aires, 1970
Anti-structure	Zodiac No. 18, Italy, 1969 Cuadernos, Suma Nueva Vision, Buenos Aires, 1970
JS in Tokyo (Interview with A. Isosaki)	Architecture and Urbanism, Japan, August 1971
'Connexions'	Architecture and Urbanism, Japan, February 1975 Casabella 399, March 1975 Architectural Review, May 1975
Asian Games	Architectural Design, January 1975
Entretien avec James Stirling	Architecture mouvement continuité, December 1975
Articles by James Stirling	School of Architecture, Zurich University, 1976
Letter from London	Oppositions 5, 1976

General articles

The work of Stirling and Gowan	A. Korn, Architect and Building News, January 1959
Two works by James Stirling, A Portrait	H. Hara and Y. Futagawa, Kohusai Kentiku, Japan, January 1965
New brutalism	R. Banham, Architectural Press, London 1966
The anti pioneers	N. Pevsner, The Listener, 5 January 1967
L'Opera di James Stirling (1950–1967)	L. Biscogli, Casabella 315, Italy, June 1967
Observations on new British architecture	T. Stevens, Bauen & Wohnen, Germany, December 1967
Pop non pop	C. Jencks, Architectural Association Journal, Winter 1968
James Stirling buildings and prospects 1950–1967	Kentiku Architecture, Japan, January 1968

Queens College, Oxford 1966/71

'The Queen's Florey Building has stolen from Keble the honour of being Oxford's standing architectural joke.

... Its style is a dialectical summary of all that modern architecture is about; emphasis is on function and structure (purpose and method) not on style and decoration . . .

Without reference to earlier styles (except possibly the architecture of ships), Stirling has made a twentieth century mark on Oxford which many people — the timid, and those who think Oxford should be all roses and wistaria — cannot take.'

Roland Jeffrey, Isis, 1 June 1973

General articles (continued)

Lettura Di James Stirling	C. Dardi, Lotus No. 6, Italy, 1969
Architecture in Britain today	M. Webb, London 1969
The politics of architecture	A. Jackson, Architectural Press, London 1969
Diz.Enc.D.Arch.e.Urb	P. Portoghesi, Rome 1969
Architecture 2000	C. Jencks, Studio Vista, London 1971
The third generation	P. Drew, Hatje, 1972
New British architecture	R. Maxwell, Hatje, 1972
Un Manierista Vinto dai Rimorsi	B. Zevi, L'Espresso, Italy, 1972
Lucky Jim	Building Design, 25 May 1973
James Stirling–5 projects	Genghia Architecture Taiwan, June 1973
Modern movements in architecture ·	C. Jencks, Penguin, London 1973
Design in architecture	G. Broadbent, London 1973
Saper Vedere L'Architettura Moderne	B. Zevi, Torino 1973
An extra dimension	N. Jones, RIBA Journal, April 1974
A modern neo-classicist	M. Girouard, Country Life, May 1974
Isometric Stirling	Design, May 1974
A detonation in glass and brick	C. Jencks, Times Literary Supplement, 21 June 1974
L'architecture dans le boudoir	M. Tafuri, Oppositions 3, 1974
*James Stirling: Buildings and Projects 1950–74	Thames and Hudson, London 1975 Verlag Hatje, Germany 1975 Communita, Italy 1975 Gili, Spain 1975 Oxford University Press, USA 1975 Futagawa, Japan 1975
reviews	R. MacCormac, Architects' Journal, 26 November 1975 E. Jones, Built Environment Quarterly, September 1975 M. Girouard, Times Literary Supplement, 29 August 1975 M. Filler, Architectural Record, October 1975 N. Ray, Architectural Review, December 1975 J. McKean, The Architect, February 1976
Transformations in style	K. Frampton, Architecture and Urbanism, Japan, February 1975
Jim the Great	G. K. Koenig, Casabella 399, March 1975
Racionalismo & Technologia	De la Ciudad No. 1, February 1975
James Stirling at IUA Congress (Spain)	Building Design, May 1975
The language of architecture	C. Jencks, Sunday Times Magazine, 10 August 1975

*Most comprehensive article

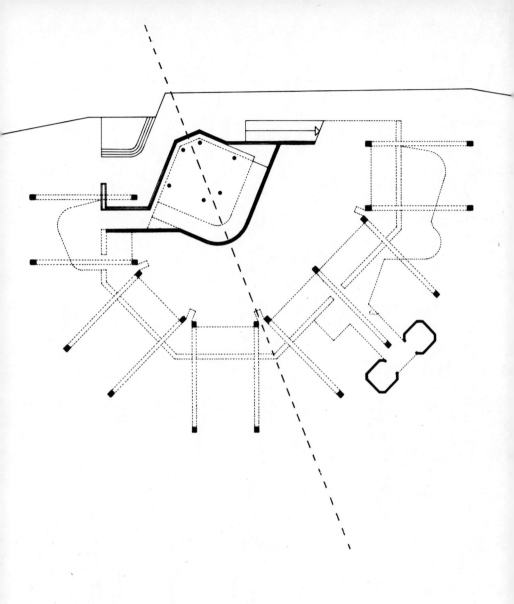

Queens College, Oxford 1966/71

Plan of structure and walls at ground level. A 45° geometry is used at junctions, with the positioning of elements on a 22½° axis. The upward sloping wall in the vertical section was designed at 11¼°.

Queens College, Oxford 1966/71

JS sketches from various stages in the development of the scheme.

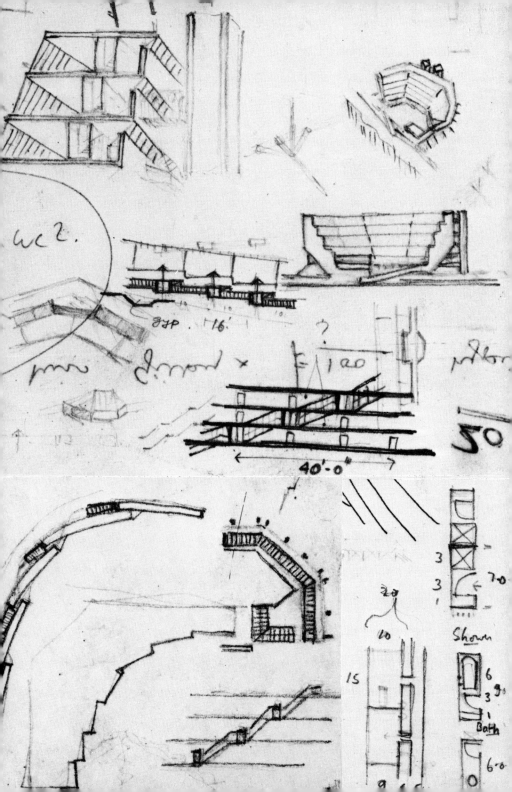

w.c²

gyp . 16

40'-0"

50

Shown

Bath

Low cost housing: Lima, Peru, 1969-

After the 'first build' by government contractor (precast RC) it is intended that the houses should be completed at ground level and upper floors added, by house owners in self building styles using traditional materials. The pride and sense of ownership achieved through self building must be retained and the inventiveness and variety of environment which this produces (in Peru) is to be encouraged and is considered essential for a dynamic community.

From the report sent with the competition drawings.

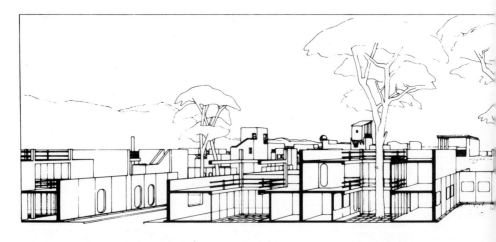

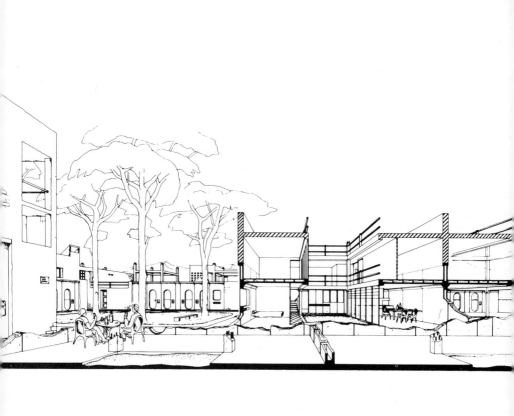

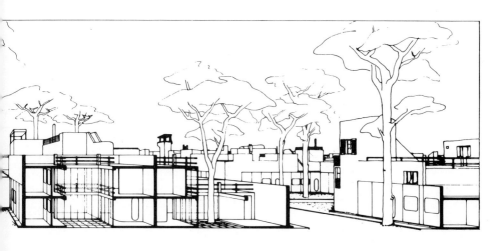

General articles (continued)

Anglo–Scottish Architect with anglo–international reputation

House and Garden, October 1975

James Stirling
(Travelling exhibition catalogue)

A. Izzo and C. Gubitosi, Officina Edizioni,
Rome 1976

Inside James Stirling

Design Quarterly 100, USA April 1976

Demythification and eclecticism

D. Stewart, Architecture & Urbanism, 1975

Articles on particular projects

Woolton House

Architectural Design, July 1956

A house which grows

House and Garden, April 1957

Ham Common flats

Architectural Journal, 17 April 1958
New Statesman, 19 and 26 July 1958, discussed by R. Banham
Architectural Design, November 1958
Bouw, September 1959
Architecture d'Aujourd'Hui, December 1959
*Domus, July 1960
Bauen & Wohnen, March 1962
Architektur & Wohn Form, February 1967
N. Pevsner, The Buildings of England: Surrey

Isle of Wight House

*Architectural Review, April 1958
Architectural Journal, 24 and 31 July 1958. House near Cowes,
J. M. Richards, 28 August 1958
Architectural Design, September 1958

House Conversion, Kensington

*Architectural Review, March 1960
Architect and Building News, 20 July 1960

Preston housing

Architectural Journal, June 1961
Architectural Design, July 1961
*Architectural Design, December 1961
Casabella Continuita, February 1962
Architect and Building News, March 1962
New Statesman, 9 February 1962, Hoggartsborough, R. Banham
Architectural Forum, March 1962
Architecture d'Aujourd'Hui, November 1962

Churchill College

Cambridge Review, 31 October 1959, The Blenheim of the
Welfare State, C. Rowe

School Assembly Hall,
Camberwell

Architectural Journal, September 1962
Architectural Design, March 1963
Architect & Building News, 18 March 1964
*Domus, June 1964
Arquitectura 67, July 1964
L'Architectura 116, June 1965

Selwyn College, Cambridge

Architectural Review, January 1961
Bauwelt, February 1963

*Most comprehensive article

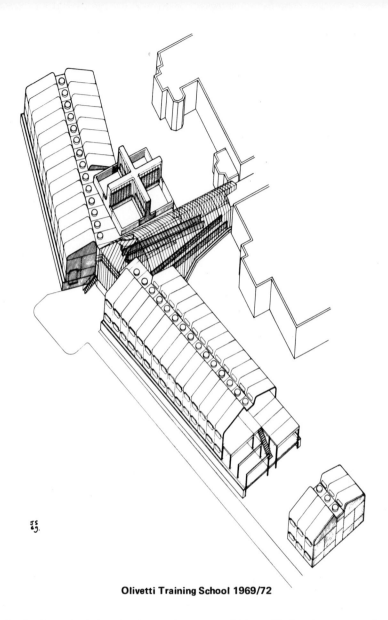

Olivetti Training School 1969/72

Each wing has been sited along level ground contours which could allow future expansion to take place. Both wings are constructed of prefabricated assembled parts and each wing can be independently extended to any length. This need for a rapid future expansion was a priority of Olivetti's requirements. The classroom wings are made of glass reinforced polyester (GRP) wall/roof units which were transported via road to the site and quickly erected. This clip together method of building is somewhat similar to Olivetti's own production of office machines and equipment.

Drawing lent by the Victoria & Albert Museum

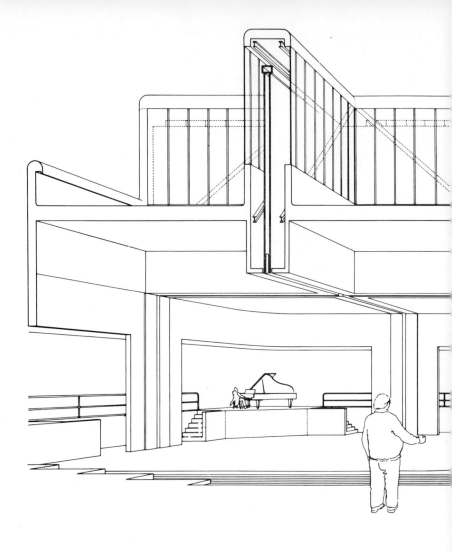

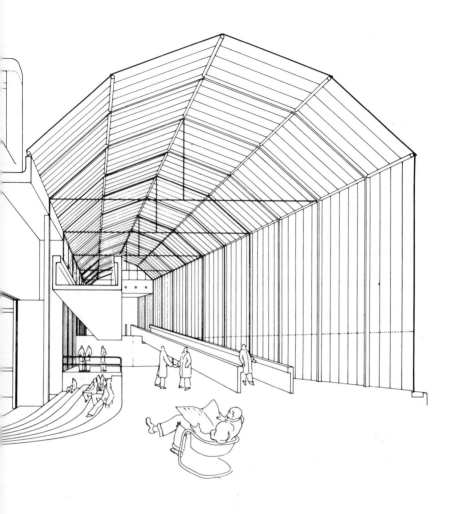

Olivetti training school 1969/72

The motorised 'roll around' walls which enclose two sides of the multispace can be withdrawn to the furthermost diagonal corners, thus opening the multispace into the circulation area of the glazed link. This enlarged area can be used informally for dances, exhibitions and film shows (the steps down into the multispace being used as seats). The 'lift up' walls which are in housings on the roof, can be lowered into the multispace sub-dividing it into four independent audio-visual teaching rooms. When various 'lift-up' walls (stage equipment) are raised, the multispace can be divided as either two or three separate rooms or further undivided into a single space lecture theatre.

71

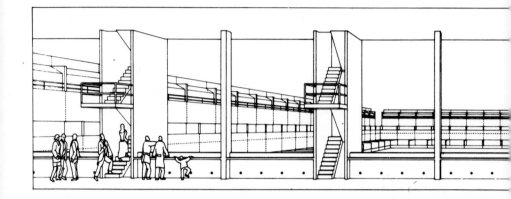

Articles on particular projects (continued)

Engineering Building, Leicester University	Architectural Design, October 1962, work in progress Sunday Times Colour Supplement, 27 September 1963, Frontiers of inner space, R. Maxwell Architectural Association Journal, December 1963 Architectural Journal, 15 January 1964 ***Architectural Design, February 1964 discussed by K. Frampton** New Statesman, 14 February 1964, Style for the job, R. Banham Architectural Review, April 1964, discussed by J. Jacobus Domus, June 1964, Un Episodia Inglese, J. Rykwert Arquitectura 67, July 1964 Architectural Forum, August 1964 Fortune Magazine, October 1964, Ten buildings that point to the future Architektur Heute, October 1964 Bauwelt 43, October 1964 Kokusai Kentiku, January 1965 Bauneister, December 1968, Glaeserne Grossform, P. Peters Architecture d'Aujourd'Hui, July 1965 N. Pevsner The Buildings of England: Leicestershire Global Architecture, ADA Edita, Tokyo, 1971 Oppositions 4, 1974, Real and English, an analysis by P. Eisenman
Old People's Home, Blackheath	***Architectural Review, May 1965** New Statesman, 23 April 1965, Form Fuddles Function, R. Banham Architettura, June 1965, Una Casa Per Anziani, R. Pedio Werk, March 1967

*Most comprehensive article

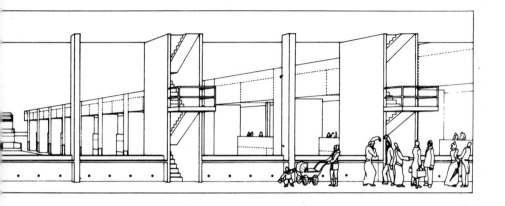

Runcorn New Town housing 1967-

The terraces of housing form a series of residential garden squares that vary in size and also degree of enclosure and outlook (the out-door rooms of the city; the idea of Bath, Edinburgh, etc.). All are tree planted and landscaped and contain children's play areas and the larger squares have tennis courts. These garden squares are for the use of the families which live around them and entry is either off the access road or via a pedestrian ramp which rises from the square, to connect with public footways at second floor level. Pedestrians using the elevated footways are connected by bridges to the town centre building at the main level of shopping and entertainments. These walkways are continued south and west out of the site to link with adjoining housing areas.

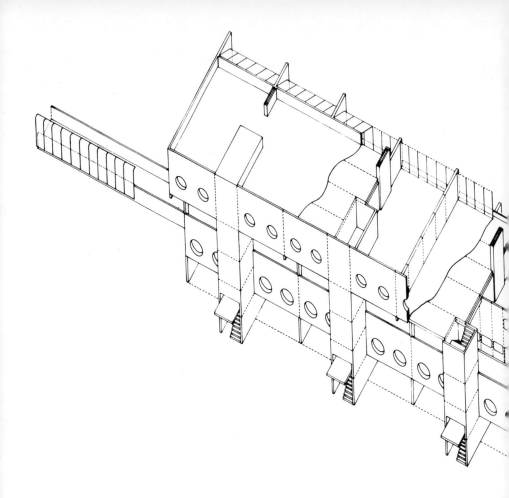

Runcorn New Town housing 1967-

An industrialised method of construction (heavy pre-cast concrete structural walls) was developed to allow off site pre-fabrication. The non-structural walls flanking the pedestrian footways where there is close tactile contact are GRP (glass reinforced polyester) in differing colour combinations related to the identity of particular squares.

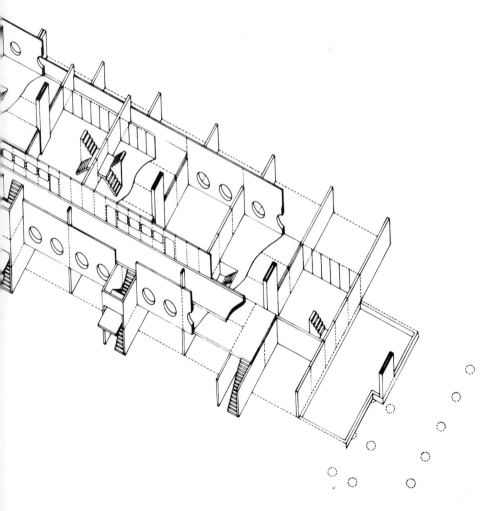

Articles on particular projects (continued)

Ch`'`dren's Home, Putney

*Architectural Design, September 1965
Deutsche Bauzeitung, August 1966
Werk, March 1967

History Building,
Cambridge University

Architectural Design, May 1964
Architectural Review, June 1964
Kokusai Kentiku, January 1965
Architectural Review, January 1965
Architectural Design, January 1965
*Architectural Design, October 1968, Stirling Dimostrationi,
A.Boyarski
Architectural Forum, November 1968, discussed by K. Frampton
Architectural Review, November 1968, discussed by R. Banham
Cambridge Review, 11 October 1968, H. Brogan
New Society 313, September 1968, Cambridge Mark II, R. Banham
Deutsche Bauzeitung, February 1969, discussed by Baete
Domus, 18 February 1969, Stirling in Cambridge, J. Rykwert
New Statesman, 18 April 1969, Virtuoso Architecture, N. Silver
Zodiac 18, 1969
P. H. Booth and N. Taylor, Cambridge New Architecture, 1970
N. Pevsner, The Buildings of England: Cambridgeshire
Global Architecture, ADA Edita, Tokyo, 1971
Cambridge Review, 30 January 1976 and
Building Design, 19 March 1976, G. Stamp
(subsequent issues of Building Design contain follow up
letters and articles)

Students' Residences,
St Andrew's University

Architectural Design, July 1966
Architektur & Wohnform, October 1966
Bauwelt, October 1966
Architectural Design, December 1966
L'Architettura No. 135, 1967, discussed by C. Assunti
Observer Colour Supplement, 31 May 1969, discussed by J. Hillman
Zodiac 18, 1969
*Architectural Design, September 1970, discussed by K. Frampton
Architectural Forum, September 1970, Semiological Analysis, C. Jencks
Domus, November 1970, Stirling in Scozia, J. Rykwert

Dorman Long

Architectural Design, July 1966
Bauwelt, August 1966
Architektur & Wohnform, January 1967
L'Architettura No. 135, 1967, discussed by C. Assunti

New York Report

Lotus No. 6, 1969
Architectural Design, December 1969

Florey Building,
Queen's College, Oxford

Architectural Design, October 1968
Sunday Times, 21 July 1968, College of Windows, N. Taylor
Space Design 11, Japan, November 1971
Architecture & Urbanism, Japan, November 1972
Domus, November 1972, Stirling in Oxford, J. Rykwert
*Architectural Review, November 1972, discussed by M. Girouard
Architecture Plus, February 1973, discussed by R. Maxwell
Building Design, 23 June 1973, discussed by S. Campbell
Isis, 1 June 1973, Florey Building, R. Jeffrey
Bauen & Wohnen, March 1974
Casabella 399, March 1975

Runcorn New Town Housing

Domus, November 1972
Architecture & Urbanism, Japan, May 1973
Casabella 399, March 1975
Lotus 10, Autumn 1975
Architectural Record, USA, February/March 1976
Domus, June 1976
*Architecture & Urbanism, Japan, July 1976
Architectural Review, November 1976
Oppositions 7, A critical assessment by W. Seligman
Architecture d'Aujourd'Hui, October 1976

Lima Peru, Housing

Architectural Design, April 1970

*Most comprehensive article

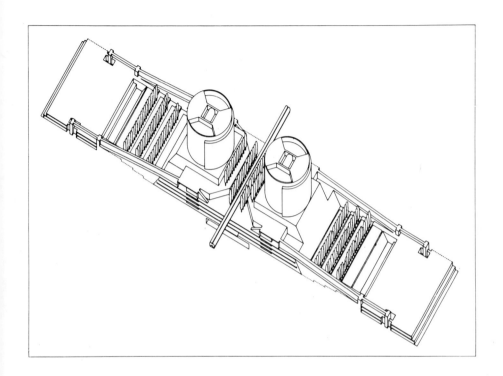

Siemens AG, Munich HQ 1969

The new complex is planned on linear principles so that incremental expansion can take place (two twin towers being the smallest module of expansion).

A travelator (enclosed moving pavements, 'people mover' e.g. Amsterdam Airport) moving in both directions, connects the new building with the S-Bahn and U-Bahn subway stations.

. . . the travelator passes down the social valley between the rows of office towers with set-down and pick up escalators, corresponding to the plazas between towers.

From the report sent with the competition drawings.

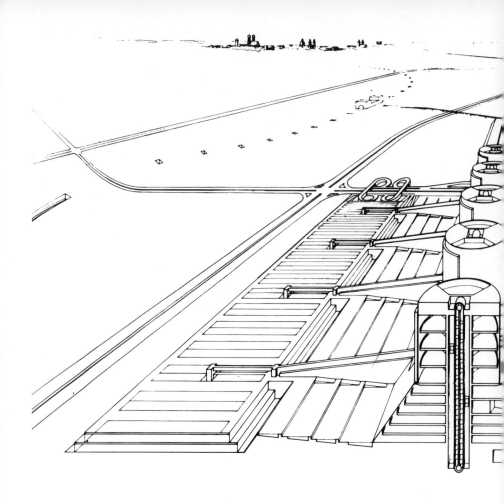

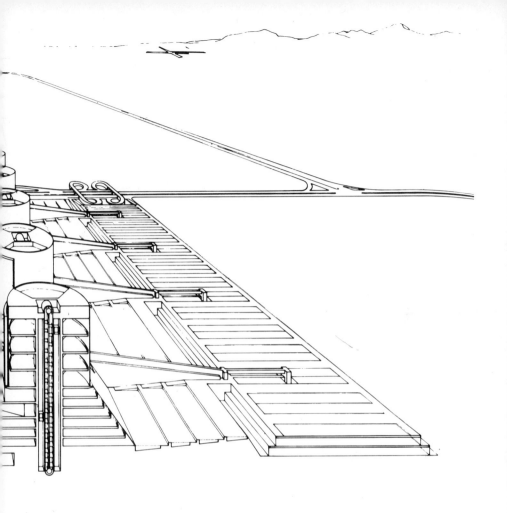

Siemens AG, Munich HQ 1969

The podium building is of six storeys and has a central core of computer research and development with the production hall at the lowest level; above this are service roads and the car park.

. . . Above are two floors of computer research and above this is the outside 'flat-top' social valley flanked by colonnades containing the social and amenity functions. This elevated pedestrian boulevard, which faces south, is lined with trees and is an important feature of the new building; although a minor element in the brief, the social requirement has become a major factor in the solution. Within the colonnades are restaurants, snack bars, news agents, tobacconists, drug stores, etc, and at the level above are social and public relation rooms. The walls of the office towers are glazed and outside there is a full height revolving sun screen, computer programmed to the hours of the day with variable louvres adjusting to the strength of sunlight.

From the report sent with the competition drawings.

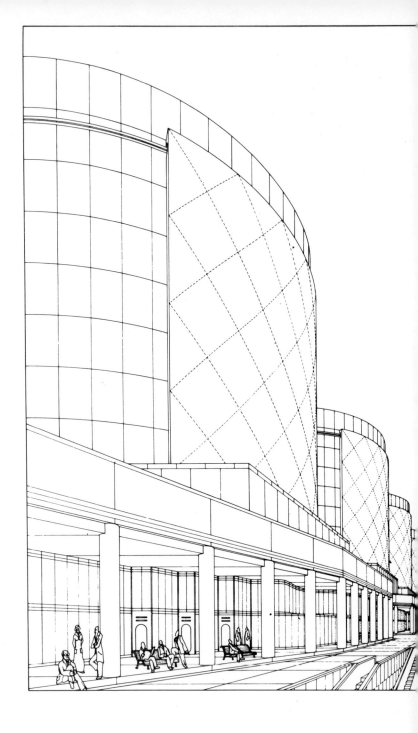

Siemens AG, Munich HQ 1969

Articles on particular projects (continued)

Olivetti Training School	Domus, November 1972
	Building Design, 22 June 1973, Olivetti's Plastic Architecture
	Progressive Architecture, August 1973
	Architecture Plus, August 1973
	Financial Times, 6 July 1973, H. A. N. Brockman
	Domus, January 1974, Spazio Polichromo, J. Rykwert
	*Architectural Review, April 1974, discussed by R. Banham
	Architecture Plus, March/April 1974, discussed by C. Jencks
	Archithese II, Summer 1974, Analysis, C. Jencks
	Architecture & Urbanism, Japan, February 1975
	Casabella 399, March 1975
Siemens A G, Munich	Deutsche Bauzeitung, May 1970, discussed by H. Hollein
	Architectural Design, July 1970
	Space Design 10, Japan, 10 October 1970
Derby Civic Centre	Space Design 11, Japan, November 1971
	Domus, November 1972
	Architectural Review, November 1972
	Milan Triennale XV Catalogue, 1973
Olivetti Headquarters, Milton Keynes	Architectural Review, April 1974
	Architecture & Urbanism, Japan, February 1975
	Casabella 399, March 1975
	Arquitecturas 8, July 1975
Arts Centre, St Andrew's University	Architecture & Urbanism, Japan, February 1975
	Casabella 399, March 1975
	Architects' Journal, 16 July 1975
Museum for Northrhine–Westphalia, Dusseldorf	RIBA Journal, March 1976, Stirling in context, K. Frampton
	Catalogue of '9 Architects' Exhibition, Dortmund, June 1976
	Architecture & Urbanism, Japan, July 1976
	Catalogue, Venice Biennale, 1976
	Architectural Review, November 1976
Wallraf–Richartz Museum, Cologne	Catalogue of '9 Architects' Exhibition, Dortmund, June 1976
	Architecture & Urbanism, Japan, July 1976
	Catalogue, Venice Biennale, 1976
	Domus, August 1976
	Architectural Review, November 1976
	Architectural Design, November 1976, Cologne in context, G. Shane

*Most comprehensive article

Derby Town Centre 1970

A major element — not part of the brief — which we have included in the design is the arrangement of shops and other functions along an internal shopping arcade (same width as Burlington Arcade at walking level, increasing in width higher up), and from this glass roofed arcade covered access can be made to the principal accommodation i.e. banquet halls, auditorium, bars, art gallery and offices etc.

From the report sent with the competition drawings.

Biography

Born: Glasgow (1926) of Louisa Frazer and Joseph Stirling.
Family moved to Liverpool in 1927.
Father was a Marine Engineer sailing from Liverpool.

⋅Quarry Bank High School, Liverpool until 1941.
Liverpool School of Art 1942.

War Service: D Day Landing.

Liverpool University, School of Architecture, 1945-50 Dipl Arch
(dist) (student exchange to USA worked for O'Connor and
Kilham in New York for five months).
School of Town Planning and Regional Research, London
1950-52.

Senior Assistant with Lyons, Israel and Ellis, 1953-56.
Worked on Architectural Competitions and involved with the
ICA Independant group, 1952-56.

Private practice from 1956 (Partners: James Gowan until 1963.
Michael Wilford from 1971).

Visiting teacher at Architectural Association 1957.
Regent Street Polytechnic 1958-60.
Cambridge University, School of Architecture 1961.
Visiting Critic at Yale University School of Architecture, USA
1960, 62.
RIBA external examiner for architectural education at the
Bartlett (London University) from 1968 to 71. Also at the
Regent Street Polytechnic from 1965.
Charles Davenport Visiting Professor—Yale University School of
Architecture USA from 1967.

Married: 1966 to Mary Shand (Sybil Sissons and P. Morton
Shand). One son and two daughters.

Honorary Member of the Akademie der Kunste, Berlin, from
1969.

'James Stirling—Three Buildings' Exhibition at Museum of
Modern Art New York USA, 1969.

BBC/Arts Council Film: 'James Stirling's Architecture' 1973.

James Stirling—drawings' Exhibition at RIBA Drawings
Collection Gallery, 1974.

'19 Projects'—Travelling Exhibition (initiated by Naples
University, and British Council 1975). Exhibited Naples, Rome,
Paris, Brussels, Zurich, Lausanne, Trieste, Tehran, Salonika,
Athens, Helsinki.

Honorary Fellow of the American Institute of Architects
from 1976.
Brunner Award, The National Institute of Arts and letters,
USA 1976.

Dortmund '9 Architects' Exhibition, Dortmund University, June 1976.
Venice Biennale, July 1976.
'Rally' Exhibition, Art Net, London, July 1976.

'James Stirling—Four Projects' Exhibition at Walker Arts Center, Minneapolis, USA, 1977.
Visiting Professor, Staatliche Kunstakademie, Dusseldorf from 1977
'Architecture 1', Leo Castelli Gallery, New York, 1977.

Lectures in Europe and USA from 1960 onwards.

Visits, lectures, etc.

1949	USA east coast (student exchange)—New York, Boston, Philadelphia
50	Paris and tour through Provence and Mediterranean Visited Le Corbusier buildings in Paris and Unité in Marseilles
55	Paris and Le Corbusier houses outside Paris
58	Tour of North Italy, Venice, Vicenza
58	Paris (with C. Rowe) visited Maison de Verre and Chantilly
60	Visiting Critic at Yale and visits to Chicago, San Fransico and Los Angeles
60	Tour of the Loire Chateaux
61	Paris (Maison de Verre) and Barcelona (Gaudi) with E. Evans
62	Visiting Critic at Yale. Lectures at Harvard, Columbia, Philadelphia, Berkeley and San Diego
64	Lecture at Berlin TU (International Symposium of Architects and Students)
64	Visiting Critic at Yale and visit to Cape Kennedy (NASA) and Florida
65	Lectures in Copenhagen, Oslo, Trondheim, Bologna
66	Tour of Greece, and visit to Mykonos. Lecture in Bologna.
67	Joint Lectures with O.M. Ungers in Rome and Naples
67	Lecture in Aachen
68	Lecture in Delft (International Symposium of Architects and Students)
68	Lecture in Stockholm
69	Visit to Lima, Peru (including Couscos and Machu Pichu)
71	Visit to Japan (with M. Wilford), Tokyo, Kyoto, Ise, Nara
71	Visit to Tuscany—Florence, Siena, Pisa, Lucca, etc (also in 1972, 1973 and 1976)
72	Visit to Lima, Peru (with F. Newby) including Couscos and Machu Pichu
72	Lecture in Barcelona
74	Lectures in Venice, Oslo, Pittsburg, Darmstadt, New York, Montreal, Tehran Tour of South Germany, visit to Iran
75	Visit to India and lectures in Ahmedabad, Bombay, Madras, Dehli, Chandigarh Lectures in Naples, Rome, Paris, Barcelona IUA Congress Madrid
76	Lectures in Lausanne, Aarhus, Harvard, Princeton, Toronto, Los Angeles, Edinburgh Santiago de Compostela, New York, Knoxville, Lexington

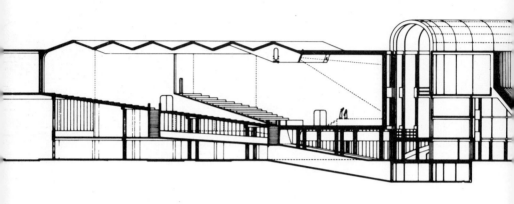

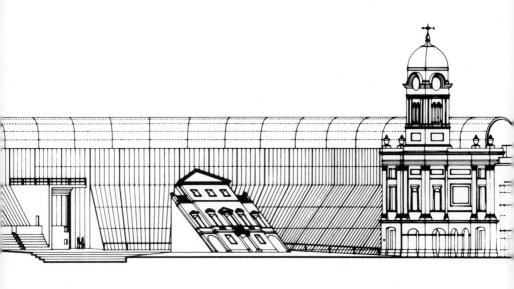

Derby Town Centre 1970 (limited competition)

'The preservation of an historic facade was suggested. Stirling tilted it back (to form a band shell roof) definitively detaching it from a former context and theatrically crashing it into another; ad hoc preservationism at its most astounding, witty and even considerate, since the facade was a familiar but not remarkable sight.'

C. Jencks and N. Silver, Adhocism

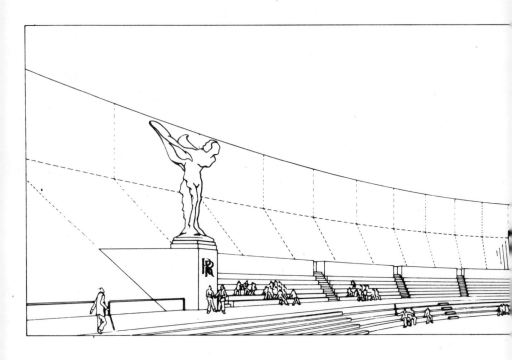

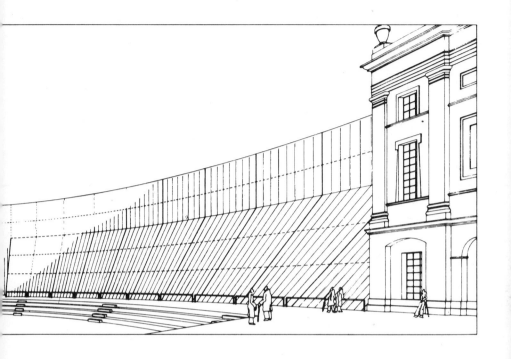

Derby Town Centre 1970

The intention is to increase the significance of the Market Place square and to achieve an entirely pedestrianised and protected area which will be the focal and most important part of the town; to create for Derby a public space which is of significance, i.e. as the Piazza del Campo is to Siena, the Royal Crescent is to Bath or the Rockafeller Plaza is to New York.

From the report sent with the competition drawings.

89

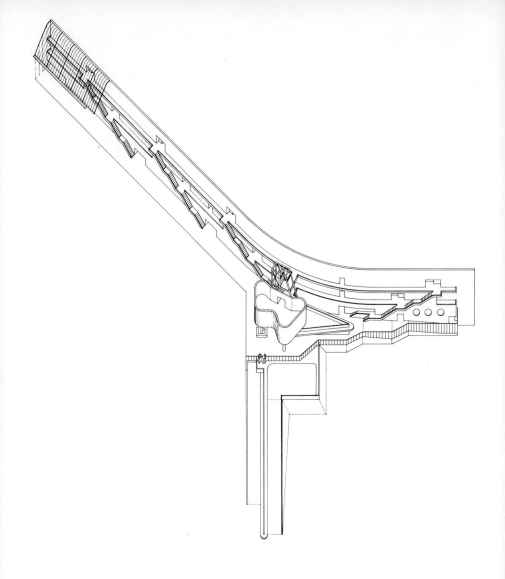

Olivetti HQ, Milton Keynes 1971-

A glazed concourse extends the length of the office building separating it from the warehouse, and providing access by means of galleries and staircases to all office and workshop floors, and also to the car park below. A conference room/auditorium with audio visual facilities is suspended within the concourse directly above the main entrance to the building and this is served by ramp and lift.

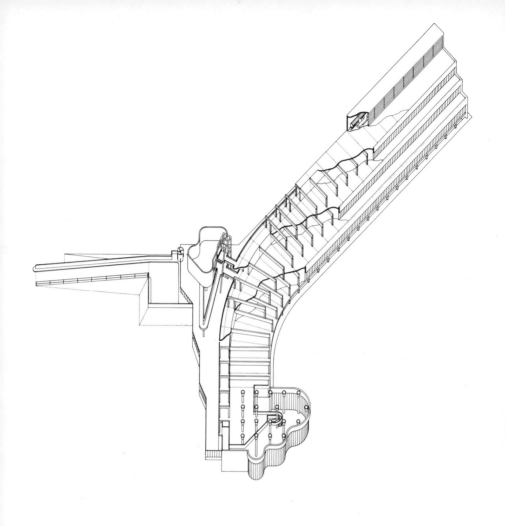

Olivetti HQ, Milton Keynes 1971-

Three floors of air-conditioned and open plan offices are arranged over a sub basement car park. The offices open onto terraces overlooking the lake and are separated from the concourse by a continuous service zone containing toilets, locker rooms, tea areas, ducts, etc. In order to reduce circulation and disturbance to a minimum within the office areas, access to the service zone is via the galleries overlooking the concourse.

Separate vehicle access is provided to the restaurants, recreation facilities and boating club located at the southern end of the office building, so that the social facilities can be used in the evenings and at weekends.

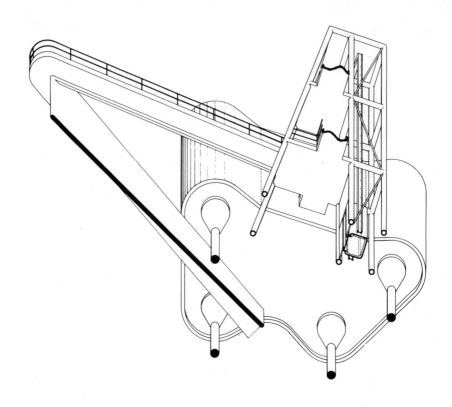

Olivetti HQ, Milton Keynes 1971-

Conference room/auditorium/audio-visual centre.

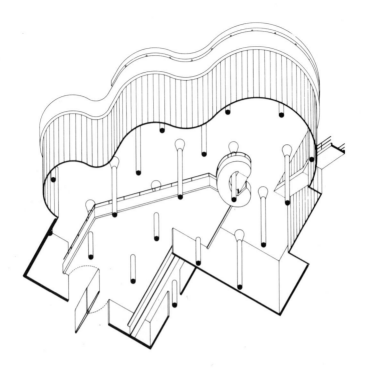

Olivetti HQ, Milton Keynes 1971-

Restaurant/canteen/social club.

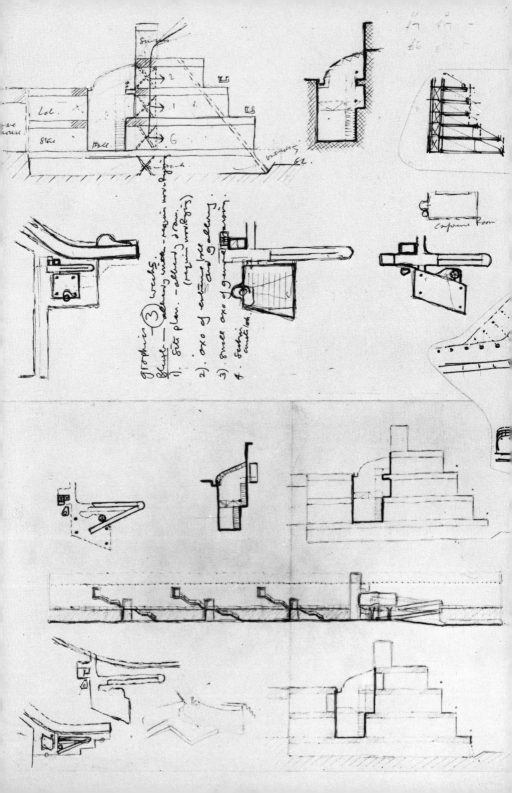

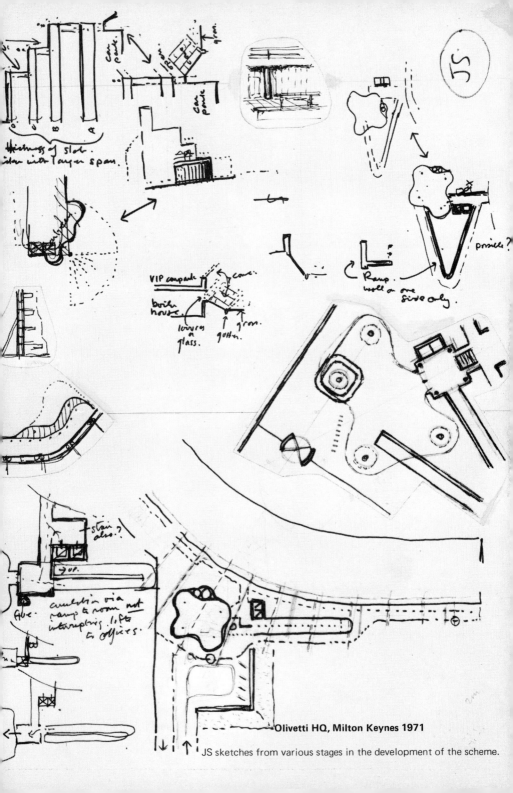

Olivetti HQ, Milton Keynes 1971

JS sketches from various stages in the development of the scheme.

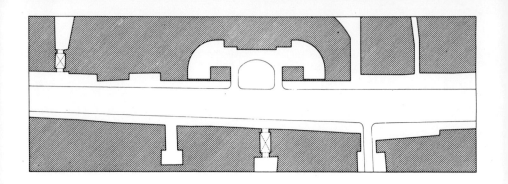

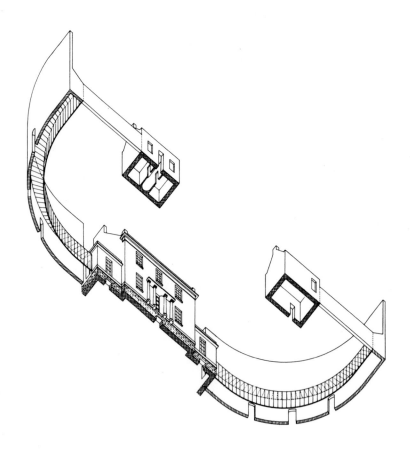

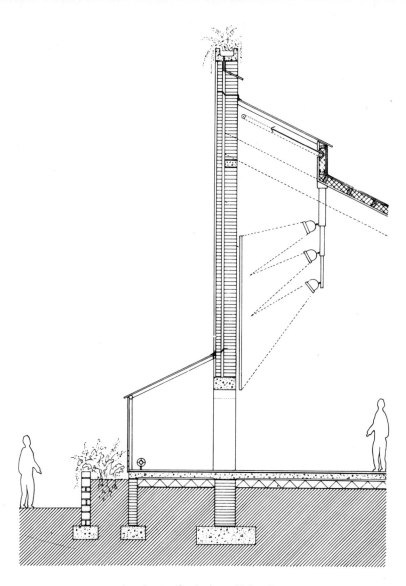

Arts Centre, St. Andrews University

'The idea of the city as a collage of "types" lay behind the rational architecture conference (March 1975)... on display in the exhibition was his tiny project for an art gallery for St. Andrews, which collaged together three existing buildings, using a curved wall to create typical internal exhibition spaces and an external entry courtyard . . . This collage technique, like townscape, can include historic fragments of popular conceptual reactions to a building or city. It destroys the total design, 'machine aesthetic' of the Bauhaus but retains ideal types.

G. Shane, The Architects' Journal, 16 July 1975

TWO GERMAN PROJECTS

These schemes are for specific buildings that fit into restricted urban places and it was necessary to show how they would alter/affect adjoining areas. In both designs we sought to reinforce particular characteristics of the site — (important urban centres in Dusseldorf and Cologne) and the building solutions are supportive of existing urban contexts.

Dusseldorf

(extracts from Architect's Report)
Re-Design of the Grabbeplatz and a building for Northrhine-Westphalia Art Collection

The following two projects have been completed since the RIBA Drawings Exhibition (1974).

'It is intended that an urban square be created on the Grabbeplatz in connection with existing buildings.'

The new Museum (Modern Art) is intended to be both a 20th Century container for contemporary works of art and an integral element in historic Dusseldorf. The design of the new building is meant to harmonise the diverging forms of the St. Andreas Church silhouette, the monumental Land-Court building, the domestic scale houses along Neubruck Strasse and the civic buildings on Heinrich Heine Alle. In addition to this (perhaps impossible) task it is hoped to achieve an architectural appearance that is as individual as the older buildings in contrast to the oversimplified appearance and overblown scale associated with modern architecture (i.e. the box; — the slab).

'The Grabbeplatz design shall be one of the essential criteria for the plan. The existing buildings shall be taken as the basis for the northern boundary of the square. Regarding this it is suggested that parts of the facade of the former town library on the premises of which the new Gallery is going to be erected may be integrated into the new building or moved to some other location.'

Only the south west corner facades of the old Library are retained where the appearance in Neubruck Strasse is important for that street. Nevertheless our attitude to the surrounding urban context is to infill and to preserve. All facades in Neubruck Strasse and Heinrich Heine Alle

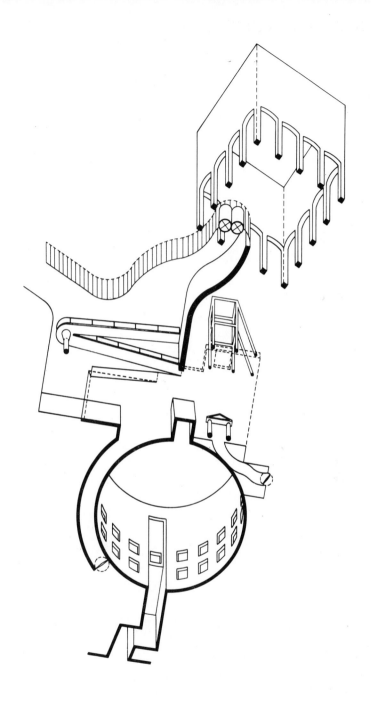

are retained, without comprising the functional working of the new building.

The Grabbeplatz will continue to be surrounded on three sides by existing roads, consequently we have raised the plaza to protect its environment from motor traffic (increasing its potential for outdoor exhibitions etc). This raised platform allows for an increased pedestrian scale (i.e. relative to the height of the Land-Court building) and a less costly carpark (reduced excavation), and its height allows connection to the municipal art gallery across the road via a footbridge.

> 'A second square should be formed in the internal area of the city block and face the north side of the Gallery and be accessible via a public passage through the building from the Grabbeplatz . . . This is intended to revive a historic connection for pedestrians from the Ratinger Mauer to the Grabbeplatz along the routing of the Old Town wall.'

To the north the Grabbeplatz is extended with a pedestrian walkthrough to Ratinger Mauer and this walk is enhanced by a series of architectural events which include a reference to the Old Town wall and a circular garden with enclosing curved wall and modulated paved surface that contrasts with the irregular edges and regular paving of the Grabbeplatz.

The pavilion on the plaza is sited on the axis of Muhlen Strasse and it marks the entrance to the new Art Gallery, the start of the Ratinger Mauer walkthrough and the way down to the underground carpark. It is also a sheltered area for those waiting for buses and coaches, provides a place for people to congregate and is, perhaps, a much smaller scale alternative to the entrance steps of the Metropolitan Museum, (New York) or the portico of the British Museum, (London). As an object the pavilion has a similar relationship in the Grabbeplatz as the Schlossturm has in the Burgplatz. It makes reference to the small freestanding building (the original art gallery) which in previous times was sited in the Grabbeplatz and has a relationship to the pavilion corners of the adjacent Land-Court building. There is also an association with the neo-classical gate houses which mark the entrance to

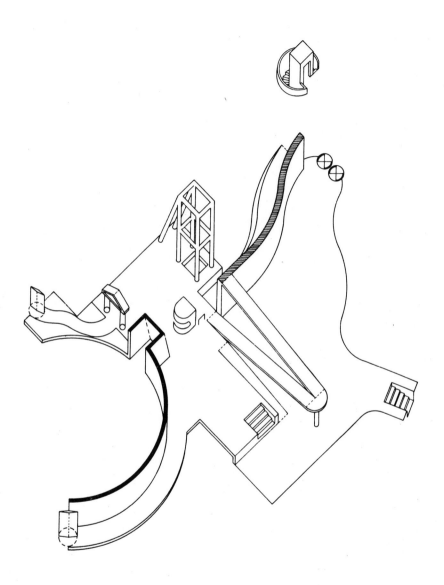

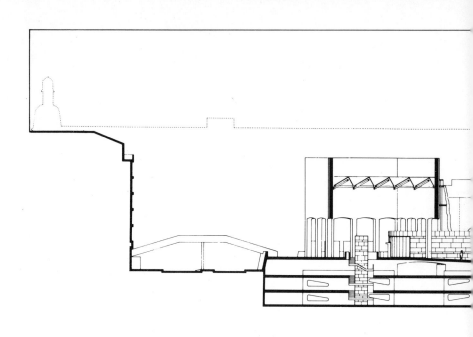

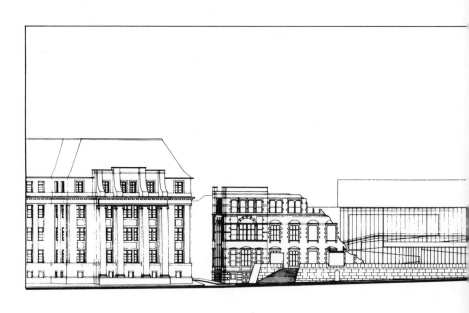

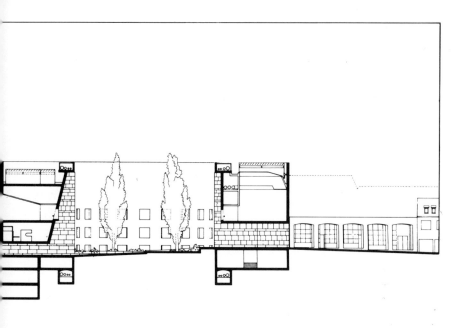

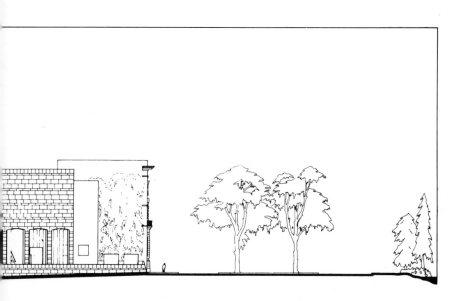

Museum for Northrhine-Westphalia 1975

the park from Heinrich Heine Alle. The Pavilion would
have a glass roof — using diffusing glass and the covered
area beneath would be flooded in shadowless light.

Entrance level

'The entrance hall is to be generously arranged since here the
visitors are offered a variety of information. This area should
be arranged as attractively, lively and openly as possible . . .
The inner entrance area is to be separated from the outer entrance area by the box office which is at the same time the
delineation of the security area.'

The protruding vestibule to the outer entrance hall has a
slightly ramped floor rising ½ metre from the plaza. This
vestibule is paralleled by the pedestrian walkthrough to
Ratinger Mauer and is defined by a continuous wall on
the site? of the Old Town wall. The raised entrance area is
approached by ramp or stairs (rising 1 metre) and beyond
the control desk (box office) is the security zone and
inner entrance area from which there is direct entry to
the Kunsthalle or access by ramp and lift to the gallery
floor above.

The lean-to glazing of the entrance hall (with no
penetration of sunlight into the galleries) produces an
irregular three dimensional space which contrasts with
the regularity of the main galleries.

Entry to the Kunsthalle is signalled by a portico
(Tuscan) and is through a 2 metre wide tunnel the surface of which could be redecorated to introduce each
exhibition.

Gallery level

Art previous to 1945
("Classics") comprising 80 medium sized works.

Art after 1945
("Modern art") comprising 40 partly rather large sized works.

Paul Klee
91 mainly small sized works, 35 of which are drawings.

Julius Bissier
101 mainly small sized works, 72 of which are drawings.

'The collection rooms are if possible to be accommodated in
not more than two storeys. The rooms for the special collection of Klee and Bissier may be separated from the remaining

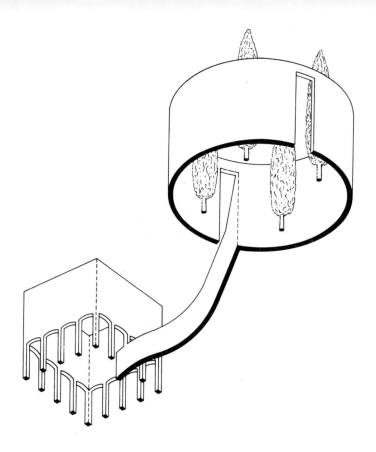

Museum for Northrhine-Westphalia 1975

' . . . Stirling literally celebrates the extension of the Ratinger Mauer, as a right of way, by creating a metaphorical city wall, through which to represent both the line and the presence of the old city mauer . . . This metaphorical wall is fully integrated into the most prominent feature of Dusseldorf; namely the entry portico on the Grabbeplatz, which not only "represents" the gallery as a whole, through its axial alignment with the main thoroughfare of Muhien Strasse, but also counters as an urban symbol the free standing Schlossturm that articulates the space of the Burgplatz, overlooking the Rhine . . . This same "empty" top lit portico—an ironic comment possibly, as to the consequence of all museum culture—also stands as a metaphor for the actual genesis of the institution, since its free standing location on the Grabbeplatz refers to the pre-war site of the original art gallery that previously occupied the square . . . This endless layering of meaning on top of meaning seems to permeate the entire structure. Thus the organic glass envelope to the entry foyer, which cascades freely down, in contrast to the frontality of the portico, serves not only to reveal the public life of the institution, but also to effect a "surreal" transition between the main mass of the gallery and the gutted shell of the library . . . Finally where the square plan of the portico echoes the square plan of the whole and where the cubic mass of the portico volumetrically inverts the cylindrical void of the circular garden, the figure ground references at Dusseldorf, attain, at least for Stirling, a level of unprecedented complexity.'

K. Frampton, RIBA Journal, March 1976

collection rooms . . . The circulation areas should as far as possible be integrated into the collection and exhibition areas . . . All collection and exhibition rooms with the exception of those for which the special light protection measures are required (Klee and Bissier) shall be adequately lighted by daylight. Rooflight is required for the large rooms.'

Public circulation would be clockwise around the circular garden if following a pre-to-post sequence. Entrance to the Klee and Bissier section is indicated by a portico (Doric) and could be through a reserve room and/or from the gallery. The two recessions in the wall surrounding the circular garden coincide with the change from pre-to-post collections (with differing ceiling heights). It is not intended that paintings should be hung on this curved wall, as the gallery walls provide the required linear surface.

The windows overlooking the circular garden provide relief and orientation for the public (e.g. The Uffizi). They are positioned low down near the floor to minimise light penetration and could be completely

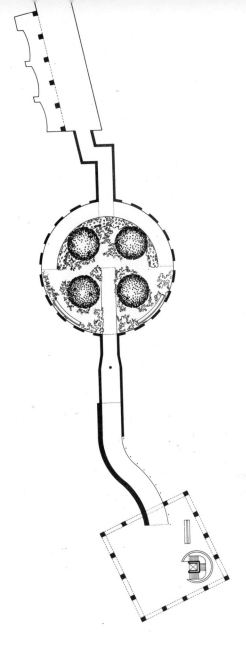

Museum for Northrhine-Westphalia 1975

blacked out if necessary. Seats/stools would be positioned with a view through these windows.

The design of the Klee and Bissier galleries provide a quite different viewing experience to that of the main gallery. The circular form with artificial lighting should make for a different incident to the pre-to-post sequence and provide an intimacy of display in contrast with the more open galleries of the main collection. A bay window (Gothic) allows the public to step off route and view the coming and going activity in the entrance hall.

(Quotations are from the programme requirements.)

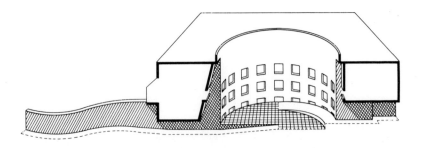

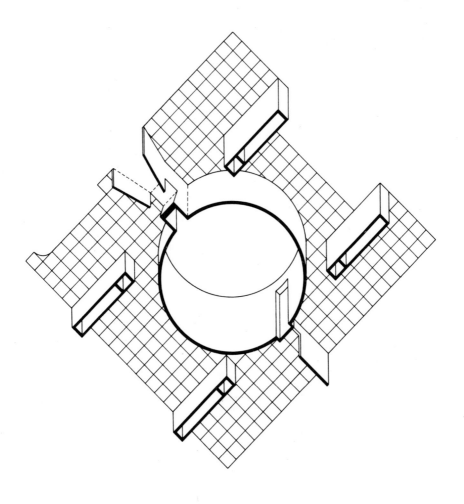

Museum for Northrhine-Westphalia 1975

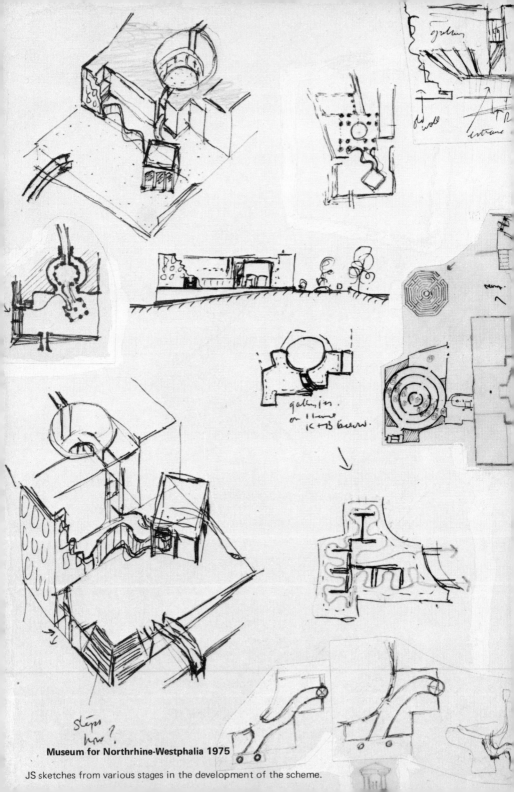

Museum for Northrhine-Westphalia 1975

JS sketches from various stages in the development of the scheme.

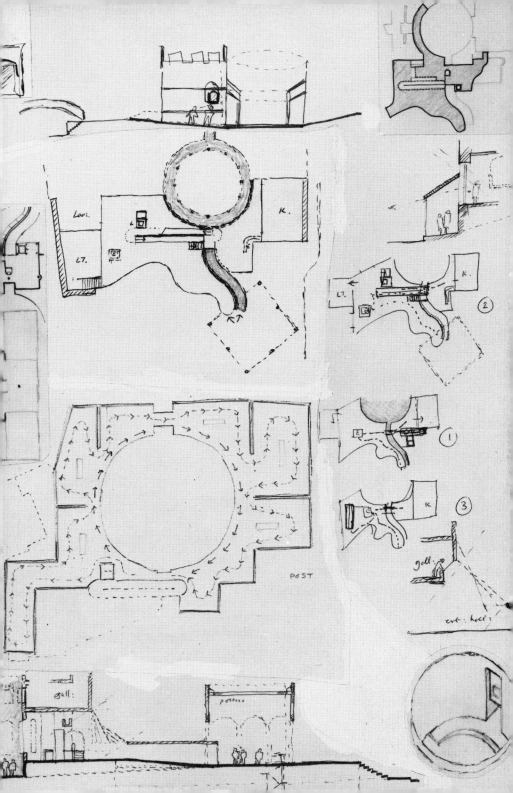

Lav.

L7.

K.

L7.

K.

②

①

E

K.

③

Jell.

ext. hall.

POST

gall.

portico

Cologne

(extracts from Architect's Report)

Development of the area between the Cathedral and the Rhine, North and South of the Hohenzollern Bridge and Railway Tracks.

'The northern part of the city of Cologne is cut in two by the large barrier of the railway installation. In the immediate vicinity of the Cathedral this barrier reaches its largest dimensions with a width of 110 metres . . . 'Despite the many advantages of the station in its present position, it is a fact that the resulting division has led to grave damage and interrupted development. Apart from occupying valuable central areas, a loss of substance of devastating effect has occured, in particular the area between the Cathedral and the Rhine still presents, despite obvious preference of location, an urban vacuum a quarter of a century after the end of the war . . . The aim of the urban project is to fill-in this vacuum with functions which use the prestigious location to "bridge" the barrier of the railway installation and to integrate the northern town centre with the city' . . .

'In the course of compilation of the project, it was found that a deck level covering the railway installation, which was at first considered a possibility, would be prohibitively elaborate as far as technical and financial problems are concerned' . . . 'It seems viable, though, to achieve a bridging of the tracks at their narrowest point at the bridgehead as well as at any other point as long as a connection is restricted to a pedestrian bridge'.

'The Riverside road will be lowered and the whole area between the river and the historical old town should be formed into a recreational and green zone. The whole project should be integrated into this zone. It follows thus that the garden area bordering the Rhine should continue upwards in stepped landscaped terraces' . . .

Our proposal for the sites north and south of the Hohenzollern Bridge is to develop them in a way that will frame and unify the separate monuments of the Cathedral, the Railway Station and the Hohenzollern Bridge, to seek integration and find an urban resolution for the railway area. The new buildings designed for both sites (Breslauer plaza to the north of the railway tracks and Museum plaza to the south) are grouped and massed in deference to the Cathedral and in response to the gateway aspect (drawbridge) of the Hohenzollern Bridge crossing the Rhine on the axis of the Cathedral. The form of the new buildings and plazas will, we hope, diminish the 'separating effect of the railway station'

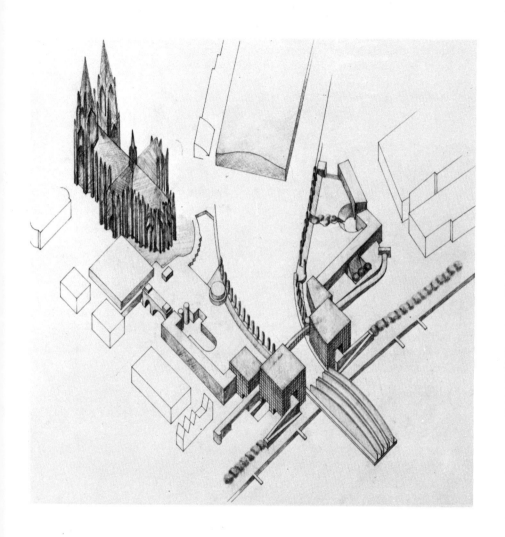

Wallraf-Richartz Museum 1975

and the 'no mans land' created by the concentration of railway tracks.

The post war construction of pedestrian plazas throughout the City has created a serious loss of geographical and historical identity between the new buildings and the memory of the old town site as it was. Even the Cathedral in its three plaza setting appears somewhat disassociated due to repetition of paved plazas and lack of contact with real ground. Therefore, at the east end of the Cathedral we suggest the removal of the terraced footpath structures in order to re-establish the appearance of the Cathedral rising freely from its natural hillside. This re-emerged 'old style' appearance of the Cathedral would dominate the east view from the new Museum plaza and the buildings designed for the Wallraf-Richartz Museum and those for Breslauer plaza are orientated towards the Cathedral. The programme suggests that the Museum site and the Breslauer site 'should be developed in several layers' and, accepting the requirement for raised plazas the new buildings are grouped around plazas which are at the same level as those around the Cathedral, thus allowing walking promenade from Dom Platz and the railway station to the Rhine edge without change of level or the crossing of high speed roads which, together with service roads, cover much of the ground surface of the building site.

Gateway buildings (monumental) are positioned either side of the bridge and, semi-enclosed within these buildings are circular plazas overlooked by museum/riveredge related shops and the esquestrian statues of Willhelm II and Friedrich which have for many years stood in the open at the approaches to the Hohenzollern Bridge are repositioned in these plazas. The gateway buildings are like civic balconies or city doors overlooking the Rhine and from them ramps incline down to the river promenade and green zone along the riveredge. On the Museum site the top four floor volume of the gateway building accommodates the multi-purpose auditorium. Enclosed escalators directly connect this auditorium with the entrance hall in the new Wallraf-Richartz Museum.

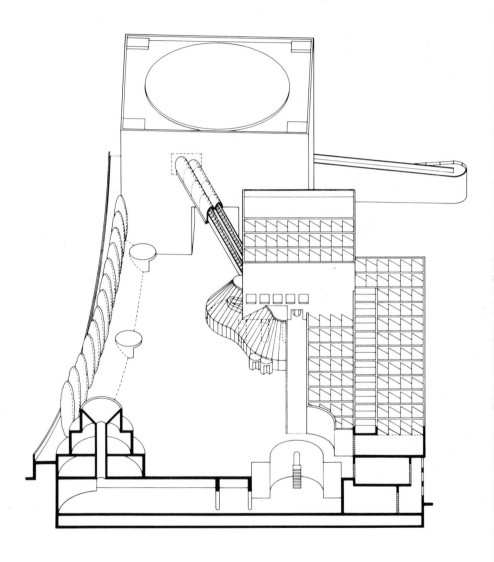

The 'no mans land' of railway tracks has been screened visually and acoustically from both Museum plaza and Breslauer plaza by retaining walls which also support elevated footpaths. These footpaths connect with those on Hohenzollern Bridge, allowing pedestrian crossing to Deutz. We have treated the edge of the railway zone like a tree lined canal bank or riveredge and the river (railway) is crossed at two places by footbridges.

Breslauer plaza is planned in a way similar to the Museum site with a plaza at 54.00m level; beneath is the bus station and carparking for 600 cars. The gateway building here accommodates a sports centre including the swimming pool in its upper levels. In the middle levels are the bedrooms of a new Commerz Hotel, most with views over the Rhine.

The north end of Breslauer plaza coincides with natural ground which is landscaped with trees, rocks, grass etc., reintroducing terra firma into the artificial levels occuring elsewhere. The plaza and the garden are separated by a ravine (picturesque) leading to an amphitheatre that could be used for public events. The six storey office building sited in this garden also accommodates the day nurseries and senior citizens club at ground level. The long six storey office building which faces over the river can be entered from the plaza via a portico (Classical) as well as from the bus station and carparks below.

On both sites the new buildings make walls which contain and define the plazas and the height of new buildings is similar to those of existing buildings adjoining, i.e. the Hotel Mondial to the south and the Bundesbahndirekton to the north. Towards the river edge the height of new buildings increases to be more in scale with that of the bridge, however this is at a point furthest removed from the Cathedral and the whole complex is subordinate to the Cathedral.

New Building for Wallraf-Richartz Museum

'The modern museum should be located at the junction of a multitude of routes used by the town population ... It should be easily recognisable from the outside and be through an adequate forecourt, easy to find . . . It is expected of the

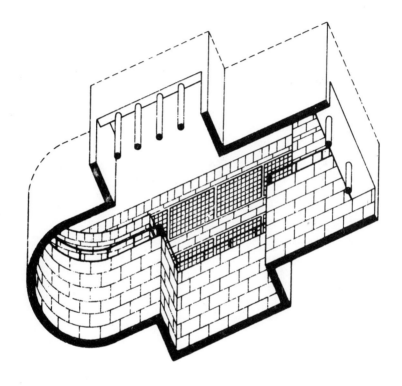

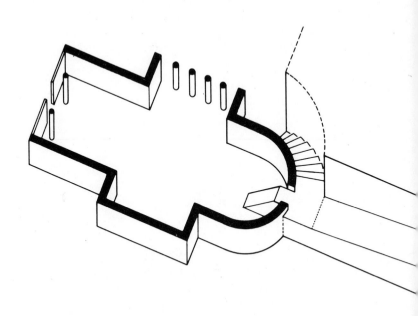

Wallraf-Richartz Museum 1975

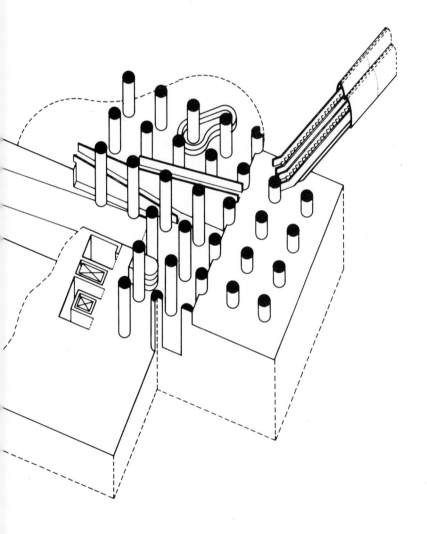

competitors that they shall work toward ensuring that the main access plane of the Museum shall consist of a pedestrian area with connections to all sides and interlinked by open and enclosed spaces and open and covered terraces . . . 'The entrance zone and surroundings of the museum are to have a special importance. This area shall evoke the curiosity of the visitor and also other museum-related shopping activities together with information facilities . . . The plan disposition should make it possible for the visitor to find particular works of art of his choice without being forced to walk through the whole museum' . . .

'The hectic changing area, as well as the quiet area, should be accessible from the neutral foyer. At this point, where the visitor has to make a choice, he should be offered not only a staircase but also a lift. It would seem to be logical in a large museum to develop the zone of change directly off the foyer, with the quite zone, however, on the upper floors. On the other hand, it might be feasible to locate the most attractive area on the upper floors, at the end of the visitor's route, so to speak' . . .

The new museum can be approached on foot from the Dom Platz and railway station on a continuous plaza at level 54.00. There is connection by lifts and stairs down to two levels of basement carparks (403 vehicles). The museum can also be approached from the Rhine promenade and river edge green zone by a large ramp which arrives in the circular plaza.

The building is in three parts; a long gallery wing; an intermediary entrance building; and the Gateway/auditorium building. The physical appearance of the plaza is determined by a series of architectural elements including a 'lean-to' entrance hall, (the shop on the corner) the sloping roof/ramp over the entrance gallery descending on the axis of a sunken sculpture court, the inclined tubes of free spanning escalators and a ziggurat (electric sub station) marking a footbridge crossing from Breslauer Platz etc.

In the outer entrance hall (peristyle) there is a large sales counter with museum information, advance booking etc. Two ramps, a down-ramp and an up-ramp, lead to separate foyers each with cloakrooms, lavatories etc.

From the upper foyer escalators rise to the multipurpose auditorium and the arrival platform serves as a balcony from which visitors proceed to three levels of viewing that are interconnected by stairs at the midpoint

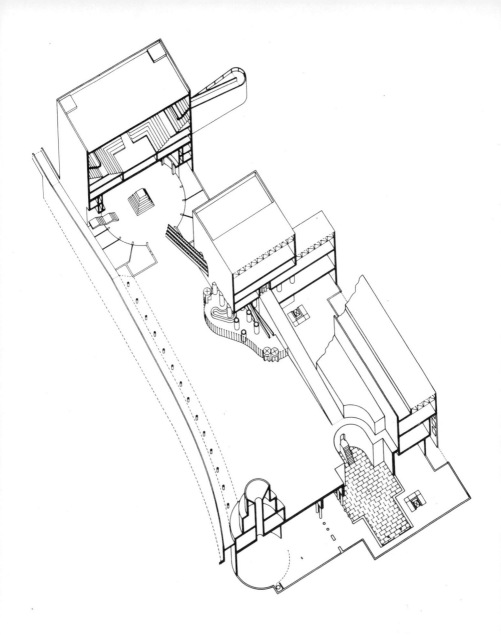

Wallraf-Richartz Museum 1975

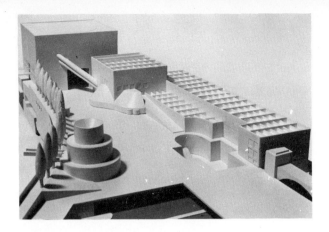

of each side. This auditorium/hall can take exhibitions, concerts, popmusic, theatre, conferences etc. On all sides there are fixed storage units (for pull-out Bleacher seating) which define a perimeter space that would be used for changing rooms, stores, toilets etc.

From the lower foyer there is entrance to the museum galleries. The planning of the galleries is such as to lead visitors along a 'preferred' route, alternatively to provide direct access (lift and stairs) for those who know what to look for. The 'preferred' route which goes via all galleries is commenced past the ticket control box and leads down a ramped entrance gallery (from which there is entry to the outdoor sculpture court) and by a shallow flight of steps around one side of the court into an interior sculpture space, off which is the changing exhibition area. This area has movable walls that can retract and open into the artists' action space allowing mutual flexibility of use.

The long gallery wing is approached via an internal passage along the West Front of the sculpture court and is planned on three levels, each with a linear arrangement of partition walls linking vertical circulation cores at either end. The partition layout of galleries varies but all relate to the principle that on each floor access is down a side lit gallery off which the visitor proceeds into larger and more flexible, top lit or artificially lit spaces.

'The parabola which Stirling has followed has a high degree of internal consistency. It indeed reveals the consequence of a reduction of the architectural object to pure language, yet it wishes to be compared to the tradition of the Modern movement, to be measured against a body of work strongly compromised by virtue of its anti-linguistic status. Stirling has "rewritten" the "words" of modern architecture, building a true archealogy of the present.'

L'Architecture Dans Le Boudoir, M. Tafuri, Oppositions 3, 1974

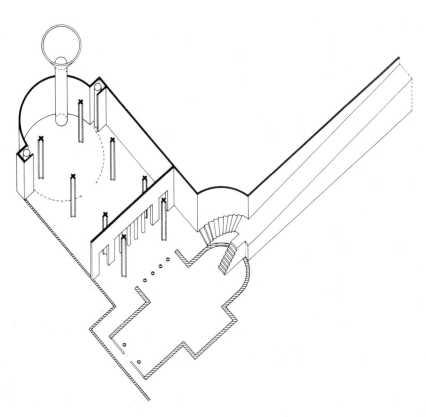

From the upper gallery (adjacent to the Restaurant which has views towards the Cathedral) there is a mechanically controlled exit door that allows departure only. Leaving the building by way of the ramp into the plaza could be an appropriate finale to the visitors' tour of the Museum; it also recalls the lead off down the ramped entrance gallery — the entry/exit procedures are similar.

The structure of the new building, plaza platform and underground carpark would be of reinforced concrete. External wall surfaces are veneered in reconstructed stone below plaza level and with natural stone above. The paving of the plaza and the sculpture court would be of natural or reconstructed stone.

(Quotations are from the programme requirements.)

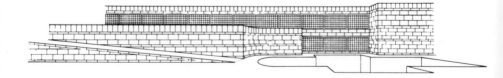

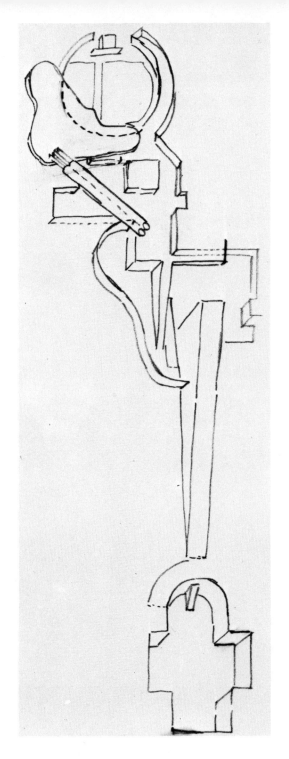

JS sketch

Drawing of JS (1972) by Ben Stirling (Age 4)